D0340300

HEART

by
SARAH R. RIEDMAN

Illustrated by
HARRY McNAUGHT
and ENID KOTSCHNIG

Original Project Editor: HERBERT S. ZIM

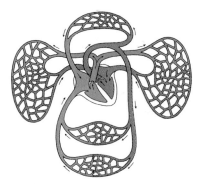

GOLDEN PRESS · NEW YORK

WESTERN PUBLISHING COMPANY, INC.

RACINE, WISCONSIN

FOREWORD

In our society where cardiovascular disease accounts annually for more than half the deaths, an appalling ignorance exists frequently even among the educated people regarding anatomy, physiology (function), chemistry, and pathology or diseases which affect the cardiovascular system. While the heart performs a vital function in the cardiovascular system, it performs one function—to pump continuously a stream of blood throughout miles of elastic conduits and supply the needs of other vital organs. Compared to the liver, pancreas, and kidneys which perform several complex functions its role is not complicated. Yet from the origin of mankind the heart has enjoyed a special and often unjustified even mystical significance. Much has been written, spoken, and even sung about the heart as a center for personality traits and emotions such as fear, courage, hatred and love, but obviously these concepts are not based upon fact. Never was this more clearly evident than in 1967 when the first successful human heart transplant was reported from Capetown, South Africa. This news was difficult for most people to understand and accept. The need for reliable and objective information regarding our bodies becomes an ever increasing necessity to cope with the rapid advances in medical science.

The advent and spectacular growth of cardiovascular surgery during the past two decades stimulated by introduction of open heart techniques has provided great interest and excitement in this new and glamorous field. Surgeons are performing operations undreamed of only a few years ago. Techniques change so rapidly, however, that even the surgeon must maintain a steady running pace just to keep up. This little book provides a convenient way for the average person to enlarge his understanding of his own body and its function. HEART is an accurate reference manual presented in clear concise style. While some of the techniques of diagnosis and treatment presented here will probably change in coming years, the factual information about the *normal* cardiovascular system will remain the same. I intend to place it at every patient's bedside!

Denton A. Cooley

Surgeon-in-Chief   Texas Heart Institute

CONTENTS

INTRODUCTION 4

THE NORMAL HEART 5

THE ANATOMY OF THE HEART 6

THE HEART CYCLE 18

HEART SOUNDS 20

HEART RATE 22

HEART MUSCLE 26

BUILT-IN COMMUNICATION SYSTEM ..30

THE WORKING HEART 38

THE CARDIAC NERVES 44

THE CIRCULATORY SYSTEM 50

BLOOD VESSELS 60

BLOOD PRESSURE 74

DEFECTIVE, DAMAGED OR DISEASED ..78

DETECTION 118

REMEDIAL ACTION 124

RESEARCH ACHIEVEMENTS 146

EDUCATION 152

MORE INFORMATION 156

PHOTO CREDITS 156

INDEX 157

INTRODUCTION

Your heart is a pump that runs continuously, without overhaul, from the fifth month before birth until death, for an average lifetime of 70 years or more. Beating from 60 to 80 times a minute, it circulates almost your entire blood supply (8-10 pints) once every minute while you are at rest. When you donate a pint of blood to a blood bank, you are giving about as much as the heart pumps in 7 beats. When you run up several flights of stairs or do a dozen push-ups, your heart increases its output 3 or 4 times. Two to 3 minutes after such exertion, it resumes its resting output. By built-in automatic mechanisms, the normal heart adjusts its rhythm and output to the body's demands. It can speed up or slow down within seconds.

Your heart is the strongest and most hardworking muscle in your body. It is about the size of your clenched fist and weighs less than 12 ounces. Its measurements are approximately 6 inches long, 4 inches wide, and 3 inches thick.

The healthy heart never tires or becomes "strained." It can restore and repair itself and is capable of the most subtle adjustments to the varying demands that are made on it. With a remarkable power reserve, it operates without a stop, and increases its strength, capacity, and efficiency with continued physical work. Moreover, as our knowledge of the workings of the heart grows and we are able to prevent or treat heart diseases and artificially augment the operation of a damaged heart, this wonderful organ can be maintained in good working condition over an increasingly longer life span.

THE NORMAL HEART

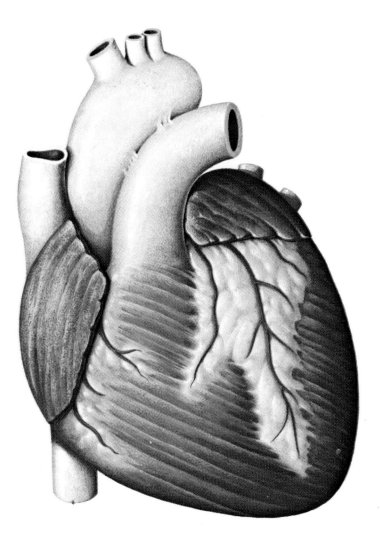

This illustration of a normal human heart is slightly smaller than actual size for that of an adult. (See p. 4 for description.)

THE ANATOMY OF THE HEART

The normal heart is a hollow muscular organ shaped roughly like a pear, with the wider portion at the top. Because of this "reversed" position, the upper part is called the base and the lower end the apex. The heart lies in the middle of the chest, between the lungs, with the apex to the left of center. During contractions the heart tends to straighten, so that the apex moves forward against the chest wall. When it is contracted, a doctor can feel the firm mass of the apex in the space between the fifth and sixth ribs.

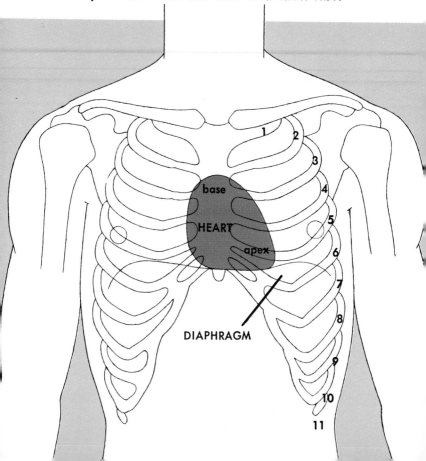

THE PERICARDIUM is a double sac that envelops the heart. The outer fibrous layer extends over the large blood vessels and merges with their outer coats; it adheres to the diaphragm and breastbone. The thin inner layer adheres to the heart muscle.

THE MYOCARDIUM, a special kind of muscle, forms the bulk of the heart. When this muscle contracts in response to nerve impulses, the size of the chambers is reduced, and blood is forced into the arteries.

A THIN FLUID between the pericardium's outer fibrous layer and the inner smooth layer acts as a lubricant. As the heart contracts inside its double sac, this fluid plus the smoothness of the pericardium's inner surface virtually prevent friction.

THE ENDOCARDIUM is made up of a layer of thin, smooth, flattened cells that line the chambers of the heart. This is continuous with the layer that lines all the blood vessels. It aids in the prevention of blood clots.

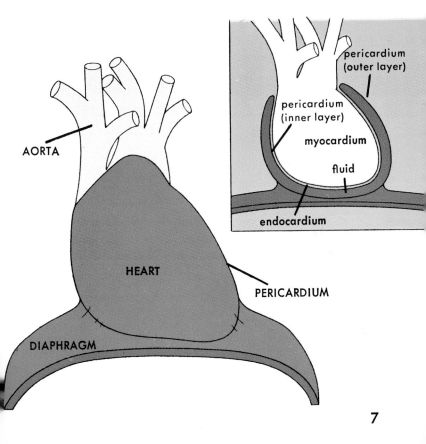

AORTA

pericardium
(outer layer)

pericardium
(inner layer)

myocardium

fluid

endocardium

HEART

PERICARDIUM

DIAPHRAGM

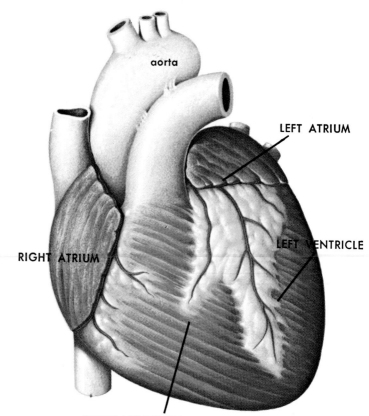

aorta

LEFT ATRIUM

LEFT VENTRICLE

RIGHT ATRIUM

RIGHT VENTRICLE

THERE ARE FOUR CHAMBERS in the human heart, as in all mammals and birds—two on the left and two on the right. Each side has an upper chamber, the atrium or auricle, and a lower chamber, the ventricle. The atria act mainly as reservoirs, receiving blood from the veins. The left ventricle pumps blood to all parts of the body; the right ventricle, only to the lungs.

THE SEPTUM, a muscular partition about half an inch thick, divides the heart into the so-called "left heart" and "right heart." The septum keeps the venous blood on the right from mixing with the arterial blood on the left. Before birth, the septum has a small opening to allow blood to flow through, bypassing the nonfunctional lungs. After birth, this opening closes.

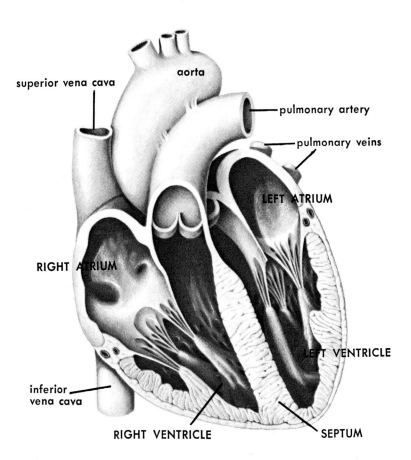

superior vena cava

aorta

pulmonary artery

pulmonary veins

LEFT ATRIUM

RIGHT ATRIUM

LEFT VENTRICLE

inferior vena cava

RIGHT VENTRICLE

SEPTUM

THE RIGHT ATRIUM receives blood from the superior and inferior vena cava—two veins that return blood from the upper and lower parts of the body—and from the coronary sinus draining the veins around the heart. This blood empties into the right ventricle, passing through valves which open in only one direction, and is pumped through the pulmonary artery to the lungs.

THE LEFT ATRIUM receives blood from the lungs via four pulmonary veins. The left ventricle discharges this blood into the aorta, whose branches extend throughout the body. At birth, the walls of the two ventricles are almost equally thick. Pumping blood around the body, the left ventricle develops five times the force of the right, and its walls grow thicker.

9

THE HEARTS OF OTHER ANIMALS vary with their degree of evolution. One-celled animals do not have a closed circulatory system and have no heart. Even in some of the lower multicellular animals, such as hydras, food is distributed without the aid of such a system. Vertebrates, animals with backbones, are the first in the evolutionary scale to have a closed system of circulation: a heart, arteries, capillaries, and veins.

Fish, amphibians, and, to a lesser extent, reptiles are so-called cold-blooded animals. At low temperatures, they are sluggish because of a low rate of metabolism. In warm-blooded animals, the birds and mammals, the arterial blood carries more oxygen than does the blood of lower (cold-blooded) vertebrates.

A FISH'S HEART is a straight, undivided tube. The aorta carries the blood to the gills where carbon dioxide in the blood is exchanged for oxygen. From the gills, the blood goes through blood vessels to all parts of the body. By the time the blood reaches the various organs, its pressure is very low. It returns to the heart through a system of veins.

AN AMPHIBIAN has a 3-chambered heart. Venous blood flows into the sinus venosus (antechamber), then into the right atrium. Oxygenated blood from the lungs flows into the left atrium through the pulmonary vein. Both atria empty into a 1-chambered ventricle, then into the conus, which divides. One vessel leads to the lungs; the other to the rest of the body.

REPTILES show the beginning of a 4-chambered heart. An incomplete partition in the ventricle and a separation in the arterial conus prevents the complete mixing of aerated and nonaerated blood that occurs in fish and amphibians. In alligators and crocodiles, the septum in the ventricles is so nearly complete that there is almost no mixing of blood.

BIRDS AND MAMMALS have a more highly developed 4-chambered heart. The conus has divided into the aorta and the pulmonary artery. Blood empties directly into the right atrium. The vestige of the sinus venosus becomes the S-A node (p. 30). In a 4-chambered heart, there is no mixing of blood between left and right sides; it is either arterial or venous.

FISH

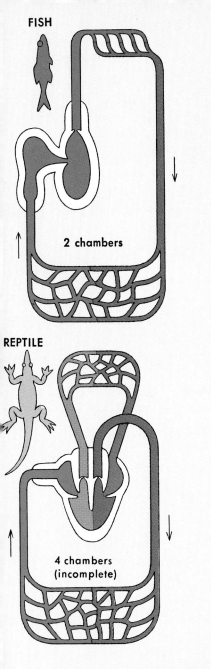

2 chambers

AMPHIBIAN

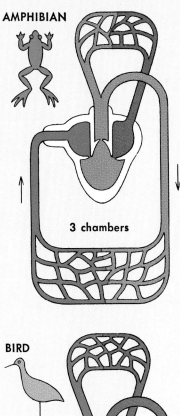

3 chambers

REPTILE

4 chambers
(incomplete)

BIRD

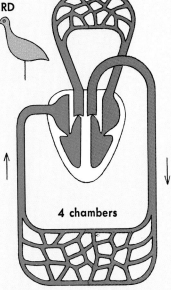

4 chambers

THE HEART AND BLOOD VESSELS make up the system that circulates blood to every part of the body. The heart drives the blood through miles of tubes of varying sizes, maintaining a continuous flow.

Circulating blood is the stream of life. It furnishes food and oxygen to the tissues and carries off carbon dioxide and other wastes constantly formed. It distributes heat generated by the cells and equalizes body temperature. It carries the hormones manufactured in some organs to other organs where the hormones regulate special activities. It conveys antibodies and cells that fight infections, and it neutralizes some toxins or poisons.

To perform these functions and maintain life, the blood must be kept circulating. If the flow of blood to the brain is cut off, consciousness is lost within seconds. If the circulation is not restored, the brain cells cease within minutes to function permanently. The heart itself cannot survive when deprived of the life-sustaining materials in the blood. Without blood, these vital organs are starved for oxygen, and life is snuffed out by accumulated wastes.

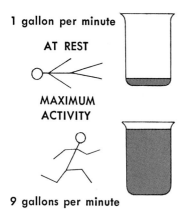

1 gallon per minute

AT REST

MAXIMUM ACTIVITY

9 gallons per minute

THE SAME VOLUME of blood is returned to the heart as is pumped out. In the course of a day, the volume of blood the human heart pumps is between 4 and 5 thousand gallons.

While the body is inactive or at rest, the heart pumps about 1/8 pint of blood per beat, or 1 gallon per minute.

During maximum body activity, the heart pumps about 3/8 pint of blood per beat, 1 gallon in 7 seconds, or 9 gallons per minute.

THE HEART IS A DOUBLE PUMP divided by a thick wall of muscle. The right half takes in used blood through two veins and pumps it to the lungs through an artery, where some of the blood's carbon dioxide is discharged and oxygen is restored. The left half receives oxygenated blood from the lungs, discharging it to the rest of the body through an artery.

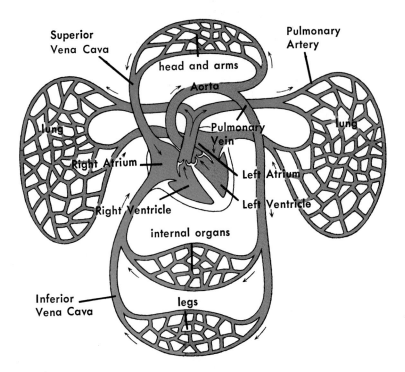

THE RIGHT SIDE of the heart, with its inlet vessels and discharging artery, is shown in blue on the above diagram. This signifies "used" blood.

The left side, with its inlet vessels and discharging artery, is shown in red, denoting oxygenated, refreshed blood.

CAPILLARIES, the connecting link between arteries and veins, are tiny, thin-walled vessels through which the exchange of gases takes place between capillaries and tissue fluid. In the diagram above arrows show the direction of blood flow to and from the heart.

CHAMBER WALLS differ in thickness. The walls of the atria are much thinner than those of the ventricles; hence, from the outside, these chambers appear smaller. This difference in muscle thickness is related to the difference in the amount of work performed by the two pairs of chambers. The atria fill with blood returned by the veins and thus act as reservoirs. However, during their contraction, they act also as booster pumps, contributing further to the filling of the ventricles. During extreme exertion, this pumping action of the atria is increased. The ventricles, on the other hand, always pump against the pressure of a column of blood in full arteries: the aorta on the left side and the pulmonary artery on the right.

The capacity of the heart varies during life and with activity, but the average capacity of each ventricle is about 4 ounces and each atrium about 5 ounces. These chambers do not empty completely when the ventricles begin to contract.

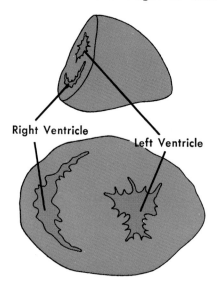

Right Ventricle

Left Ventricle

CROSS-SECTION VIEWS of the heart, exposing the right and left ventricles are shown here. Observe the difference in the shapes of the two chambers as well as the thickness of their walls. The crescent-shaped chamber is the right ventricle. Its wall is about one-sixth of an inch thick. The left ventricle is more spherical in shape, and its wall is from one-third of an inch to one-half an inch in thickness. The wall of the left ventricle is greater in thickness than that of the right because it pumps against a much higher pressure in the aorta, creating a greater workload.

THE PUMPING POWER of the heart resides chiefly in the thick muscles of the ventricles. These two pumps contract in unison because they are joined by a common partition (the septum) and are enveloped by several bands of muscle arranged spirally around both chambers. When the ventricles contract, the spiral muscle bands shorten, and blood is squeezed out of both sides simultaneously. This motion resembles the wringing out of a cloth by a figure-eight twist.

The synchronous pumping of the two ventricles ejects the same amount of blood into the two great vessels at either side. This prevents either back-up or depletion of the blood in one or the other side of the heart and insures a continuous flow of blood to and from the atria. This arrangement makes for an efficient pumping system.

Four groups of muscle fibers wring blood out of the ventricles. Two groups (A and B) wind around the outside of both ventricles. Beneath these, a third group (C) also winds around both ventricles. Beneath these, a fourth group (D) winds around left ventricle only.

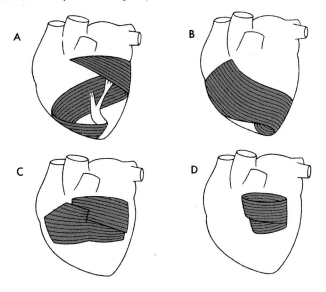

FOUR HEART VALVES consist of two sets so constructed that the blood moves always from the atria to the ventricles to the great arteries. Between the atria and ventricles are the atrioventricular or a-v valves, triangular flaps of fibrous tissue. At their base, the flaps merge into a ring of cartilage around the atrial openings. Another set of valves fits the openings that lead into the arteries.

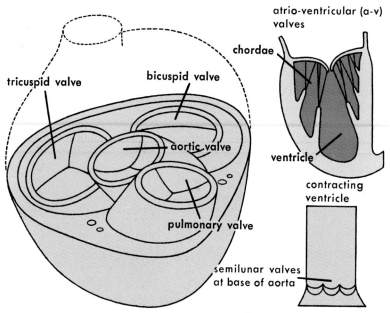

tricuspid valve

bicuspid valve

aortic valve

pulmonary valve

atrio-ventricular (a-v) valves

chordae

ventricle

contracting ventricle

semilunar valves at base of aorta

THE TRICUSPID, the a-v valve on the right side of the heart, has three flaps or cusps. On the left side is the bicuspid (mitral) valve with two larger, thicker flaps. The valves' pointed, free ends project into the ventricles, attached by stout tendonlike cords (chordae tendineae). Raised structures, extensions of ventricular muscle (papillae), mark the points of attachment.

SEMILUNAR VALVES prevent the flow of blood back into the heart from the aorta and the pulmonary artery. Each valve consists of three half-moon-shaped cusps, each attached to the artery's inside wall where it joins the ventricle. Its free end projects into the lumen (passageway) of the blood vessel. All heart valves open in the direction of normal blood flow.

When the ventricles are filling, the inlet valves are open and the outlet valves are closed. When the ventricles are discharging, the inlet valves are closed and the outlet valves are open. The valves are opened or closed by the pressure of the blood pushing against them. Pressure of the blood varies between the chambers of the heart and the blood vessels as the heart contracts and relaxes.

BLOOD flows freely from the atria to the ventricles when the pressure is higher above the valves than below. This is true during atrial contraction, when blood is being forced into the ventricles, and also while the heart is at rest and the blood drifts from the upper chamber into the lower (p. 9).

When the ventricles contract, the blood runs behind the valves and pushes their free, pointed ends together. This closes the opening to the atria. The cords attached to the valves keep them from being forced up into the atria. The papillae to which the cords are attached contract when the rest of the ventricular muscle contracts and pull the cords tight, like the guy wires of a tent. The same increased pressure that closes the a-v valves as the ventricles contract also sends the blood into the arteries. Backflow as the ventricles relax is prevented by the filling of the cupped semilunar valves. This pulls together their free edges so that they meet, shutting off the arteries from the ventricles. Because of these pressure differences and the operation of the valves, the blood moves in only one direction.

Relaxed

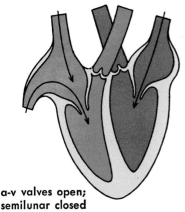

a-v valves open;
semilunar closed

Contracting

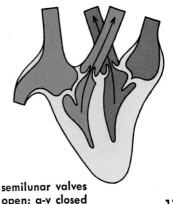

semilunar valves
open; a-v closed

THE HEART CYCLE

In each heartbeat, first the atria and then the ventricles contract in a kind of kneading motion, followed by a pause. Thus, the heart (cardiac) cycle, repeated an average of 72 times a minute, consists of atrial systole (contraction of the auricles), ventricular systole (contraction of the ventricles), and diastole (relaxation and pause). Each complete heart cycle lasts 0.8 second.

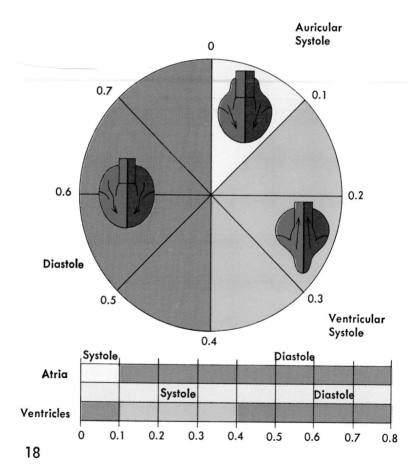

THE HEART RESTS for longer than 0.4 second of the diastole because the atria are also relaxed and at rest during ventricular systole, as are the ventricles during atrial systole. This helps to explain why heart muscle does not tire. Voluntary muscles, such as those of the trunk and limbs, contract more quickly, with only short pauses or rests between contractions.

The heart's rest periods also occur when the body is active—but they are not short enough to tire the heart. When the heart beats more rapidly, the voluntary muscles are supplied with more food, and the extra wastes are removed at a faster rate.

During diastole, the heart fills with blood. This is as important as the heart's contraction, for only as much blood can be pumped out of the heart as the heart receives. If the filling period is shortened, the heart's output of blood during systole is correspondingly reduced.

ATRIAL SYSTOLE occurs when the atria contract and blood rushes into the ventricles, which are at rest.

VENTRICULAR SYSTOLE occurs when the ventricles contract, closing the a-v valves and pushing open the semilunar valves. Blood rushes into the aorta and pulmonary artery. The atria are at rest.

DIASTOLE occurs when both ventricles and atria are at rest. The semilunar valves are closed and the a-v valves are open. Blood from the venae cavae and the coronary sinus fills the atria and drifts into the ventricles.

During the 0.8-second cycle of diastole, the atria and ventricles are at rest together for 0.4 second. But the atria actually rest for 0.7 second—during diastole, plus the ventricular systole. The ventricles rest for 0.5 second—during diastole plus the atrial systole.

THE HEARTBEAT

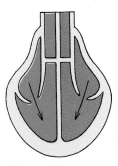

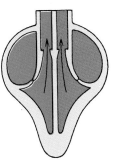

Atrial Systole   Ventricular Systole   Diastole

19

HEART SOUNDS

Heart sounds rhythmically accompany the heartbeat. You can hear these sounds in a thin person by placing your ear against his chest over the heart. You can sometimes hear your own heart sounds magnified through a pillow when you lie on your left side. But both the vibration frequencies (pitch) and the intensity (loudness) of heart sounds are below the normal range of hearing without amplification. Audible heart sounds and murmurs are shown in the graph below.

Heart sounds are produced by (1) vibrations of the contracting ventricles (the walls of the atria are too thin to produce audible vibrations), (2) snapping shut of the valves, and (3) the rush of blood. In the normal flow through the heart chambers and great vessels, the blood does not produce an audible sound. In a diseased heart, turbulence changes sounds so they can be heard.

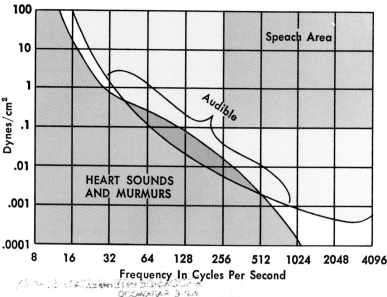

Graph shows audibility area of heart sounds.

THE STETHOSCOPE,

an instrument that amplifies and transmits sound energy to the ear, is used by doctors to listen to the sounds of the heart or other organs (lungs or stomach). Abnormal sounds can be distinguished. This process is called auscultation.

AUSCULTATION is an art as old as Hippocrates. However, the first instrument devised to augment the powers of the naked ear was not invented until 1816. Its inventor, the noted French physician René-Théophile Laennec wrote, "I was consulted by a young lady who presented general symptoms of heart disease. . . . The age and sex of the patient forbidding the type of examination (applying the ear directly to the chest) . . . I remembered a well-known phenomenon of acoustics: If the ear is applied to one end of a beam, a pin prick is most distinctly heard at the other end. I thought that maybe I could make use of this fact."

He rolled a sheet of paper into a tube, placing one end of the cylinder to the chest and the other to his ear. He was surprised and delighted to hear the beating heart much more clearly than ever before. Later he replaced his rolled sheets of paper with a wooden tube about a foot long, cupped at the ends to about an inch and a half. He named it the stethoscope. The modern stethoscope (binaural) has an amplifier and two rubber tubes, each with an earpiece.

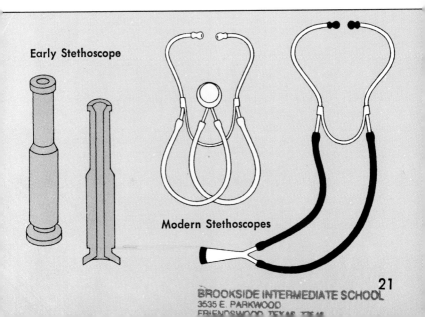

Early Stethoscope

Modern Stethoscopes

21

HEART RATE

The heart rate, or pulse, is determined by counting the heart beats per minute. As the heart spurts blood into the aorta during systole, the elastic arterial wall is stretched. During diastole, the wall recoils, squeezing the blood forward. This alternate stretch and recoil of the arterial wall passes wavelike through all arteries and is felt as a pulsation in any large artery.

In addition to the heart's rate, a doctor can tell whether the pulse is "strong," "weak," or "irregular." This is a quick way to tell the strength and regularity of the heartbeat and the condition of the arteries.

DURING VENTRICULAR SYS-TOLE, blood is forced into the aorta at maximum pressure, stretching its elastic wall. The relatively higher pressure of the blood in the aorta directly after systole forces the aortic valves closed, and the blood can move only in one direction—along the aorta *away* from the heart.

DURING DIASTOLE, the stretched aortic wall recoils, and the blood is squeezed forward along the aorta. This stretches the next portion of the artery, which also recoils immediately. Thus, a wavelike series of pulsations passes continuously along the arteries, corresponding to the beats of the heart.

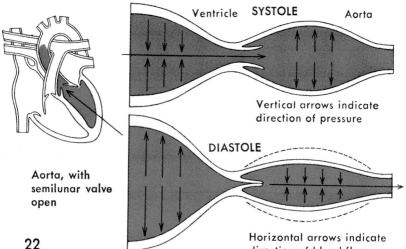

Aorta, with semilunar valve open

Ventricle SYSTOLE Aorta

Vertical arrows indicate direction of pressure

DIASTOLE

Horizontal arrows indicate direction of blood flow

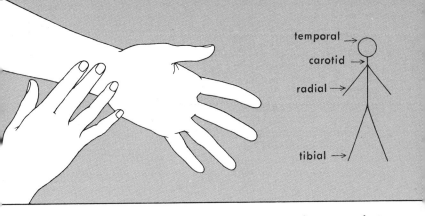

temporal
carotid
radial
tibial

You can take your pulse by pressing the first two fingers against the inside of the wrist at the radial artery. When taking someone else's pulse, be careful not to use your thumb, which has its own pulse. You can also feel the pulse in the ankle (tibial artery), or at the temple (temporal artery).

A PULSE RATE of 72 per minute is average, but like any average, it does not apply to any one person. Individual, normal pulse rates may vary from 50 to 100. For example, the rate is different when lying down, sitting, or standing. Remember this when comparing a resting pulse rate with a pulse rate after exercise.

The pulse rate also varies with sex, age, and body size. A man's pulse rate averages 7 to 8 beats lower than a woman's. In both sexes, the pulse rate de-creases with age. At birth, the pulse rate averages 130 to 150. In a child at the age of three, it is 80 to 100. After the age of twenty, the pulse rate is fairly stable, but often increases again in elderly persons. Athletes (see graph) usually have a lower pulse rate than do sedentary persons because of their more efficient hearts. A person's body size plays only a small part in determining his heart rate, but generally, the larger the person, the lower the pulse rate.

This graph shows the results of an experiment to determine variation in the heart rates of 1,000 athletes (individuals considered to be in excellent physical condition). Note that the average heart rate is 64 beats per minute.

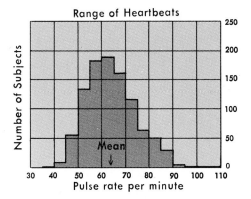

Range of Heartbeats

Number of Subjects

Mean

Pulse rate per minute

PULSE RATES VARY with different times and conditions. The pulse is lowest in early morning, highest in late afternoon—a variation that coincides with curves of temperature and breathing, even during illness. On a hot day or after a hot bath, the pulse rate may increase 10 to 15 beats per minute. Also, the rate is generally higher in the summer than during winter. The rate is 4 to 5 beats lower when lying down than sitting; a move to a standing position increases the rate by 6 to 8 beats.

Activity of the digestive organs increases the heart rate. After a heavy meal, the pulse may increase 8 to 15 beats a minute. High altitude stimulates heart action. Sudden fear generally slows the pulse. Anger, excitement, and joy can cause the pulse to "race."

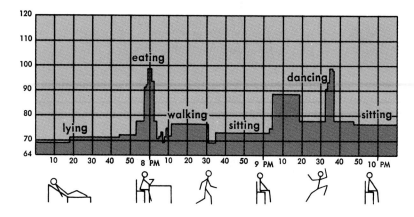

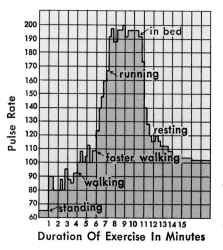

EXERCISE and strenuous effort cause the greatest rise in heart rate, proportional to the task. Running or other exercises that involve speed increase the pulse more than do pushing or pulling a heavy load. A fast run for ten minutes may nearly triple the pulse. The rise occurs within about a minute and is sustained during the exercise. When the exercise is over, the pulse begins immediately to decrease but it takes much longer for it to return to its normal rate than it did to rise.

Pulse Rate

Duration Of Exercise In Minutes

CHANGES IN ACTIVITY change the normal heart rate. The change in pulse rate from a reclining to a standing position is often taken as an index of physical fitness. A rise of less than 10 beats is generally considered an indication of good physical condition. The adjustment is made with the least possible rise in rate along with the greatest amount of increased force of beat necessary to furnish enough blood to the muscles or organs demanding the change.

In certain diseases, such as infections accompanied by fever or an overactive thyroid, the heart rate is usually higher than normal. At these times, the body cells demand more food and oxygen.

OTHER ANIMALS HEART RATES vary widely. The cold-blooded animals generally have a lower heart rate than the warm-blooded. The pulse rate of small warm-blooded animals is usually higher than that of large ones. For example, a canary's pulse is about 1,000; **an elephant's, about 40.**

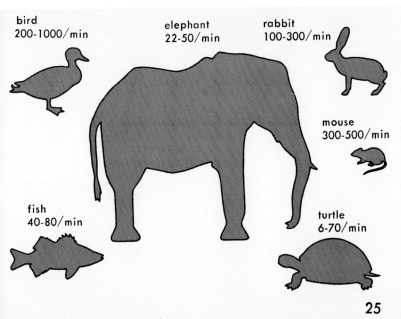

bird
200-1000/min

elephant
22-50/min

rabbit
100-300/min

mouse
300-500/min

fish
40-80/min

turtle
6-70/min

HEART MUSCLE

Heart, or cardiac, muscle is intermediate in structure between two other kinds of muscle in the body—the smooth muscle found in blood vessels and internal organs, and the striped or striated muscle of the trunk and limbs. All muscle tissue, however, consists of muscle cells or fibers. Viewed by an electron microscope, each fiber can be seen to consist of long threads, or myofibrils. When the muscle contracts, these myofibrils shorten, thicken, and stiffen.

CARDIAC MUSCLE FIBERS are about the same size as those in smooth muscle, but they are cylindrical in shape like the fibers in skeletal muscle. Each cardiac muscle fiber, like each smooth muscle fiber, contains only one nucleus. Skeletal muscle fibers contain many nuclei and are about 50 times longer than cardiac muscle fibers. Both smooth and cardiac muscle are controlled involuntarily; skeletal muscle is under voluntary control and contracts much faster.

The structural features of heart muscle are unique. Its cells or fibers branch like unravelled threads of wool. These branches interlock extensively, and this helps to spread contraction waves from one part of the heart to another. Under a microscope, the individual fibers can be seen to be so closely united that it would be virtually impossible to tell them apart if it were not for the nuclei; each nucleus belongs to a single muscle cell. The cell or fiber is enveloped in a thin membrane, the sarcolemma.

Under high magnification, cardiac muscle fibers appear to be faintly striped across their width. These lateral striations are believed to be aggregations of tiny bodies that furnish the enzymes necessary for the heart's tireless contractions.

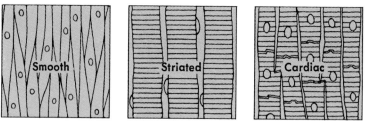

Smooth   Striated   Cardiac

THREE TYPES OF MUSCLE FIBER

UNIQUE FEATURES of heart muscle are: (1) it is "self-starting," requiring no stimulation by nerves; (2) it beats with a regular rhythm, a quality known as rhythmicity; (3) the rhythm cannot be interrupted by stimulating the heart during systole; (4) it contracts continuously without tiring; (5) under a given set of conditions, it contracts to its maximum. These special qualities were discovered by experiments done mainly on such cold-blooded animals as frogs and turtles. In suitable solution, the heart of these animals could be kept alive and beating outside the body.

THE KYMOGRAPH is used to record the contractions in such experiments. It can also be used to record blood pressure or respiratory action. This instrument is wound like a clock, and its drum is covered with a smoked sheet of paper. A thin, metal lever is attached to the heart. The opposite end has a sharp point that "writes" the beat of the heart by scratching a curve on the smoked sheet as the drum rotates. This illustrates the property of the heart called its "refractory period."

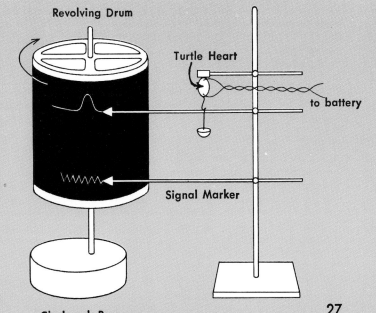

Revolving Drum

Turtle Heart

to battery

Signal Marker

Clockwork Base

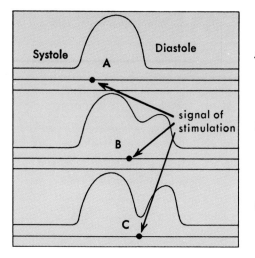

Systole | Diastole
A

signal of stimulation
B

C

A. Stimulus too weak to produce contraction

B. Premature contraction

C. Later stimulus; more complete contraction

The kymograph recordings above show that the heart muscle failed to react to an electric-shock stimulation during systole (A). When the stimulus was applied during diastole (B), the response was weak.

THE REFRACTORY PERIOD is the short interval following a muscle's contraction when it cannot be excited to contract again. In the heart, the refractory period occurs during systole. It may last for as long as 0.2 second, or most of the systole period. This prevents the heart from going into a sustained contraction, thus ceasing its rhythmic beat. Demonstrations of this sort are made by use of the kymograph (p. 27).

RHYTHMICITY of the heart (its periodic beat) is built into the muscle cells. It has long been known that an animal's heart continues to beat after the nerves that control the rate of the heartbeat are cut, or even after the heart is removed from the body. A dog's heart, for example, beats outside the body if oxygenated blood is kept circulating through it.

Recent studies with mammalian heart tissue (taken apart so that single cells could be grown in tissue culture) showed that each cell possesses the power of contraction at its own periodic rate. As the cells grow and multiply under incubation in a nourishing solution, they make contact and join together. Once completely interconnected, they beat at the same rate in unison.

In the body, the very function of the heart as a pump depends upon all the cells working together. When this coordination breaks down (a condition known as fibrillation), the heart fails to deliver blood—it no longer is a pump.

LAWS OF THE HEART reveal some interesting principles. When you lift a heavy weight, your biceps muscle contracts more than when you lift a lighter weight— *more muscle fibers* contract to lift the heavier load. But in the heart, *all* the fibers contract to a maximum with each beat. This is called the "all-or-none" principle. The heart does not expel the same amount of blood at all times, however. In fact, because of another law of physiology, the heart discharges varying quantities of blood during rest and work.

The more the heart muscle is stretched, the more powerfully it contracts—a principle known as Starling's Law. The degree of stretch is determined mainly by the volume of blood in the ventricles at systole. This blood level depends on the amount returned to the veins by the atria. Thus, according to Starling's Law, the greater the volume of blood and the more stretched the muscle, the more forceful is its contraction and the greater the quantity of blood ejected per beat. The heart, like a rubber band that has lost its elasticity, can be damaged by excessive stretching during diastole, and, subsequently, its contraction strength is reduced. The dilated heart, though filled with blood, soon fails to contract, a condition that occurs in congestive heart failure.

Heart muscle complies with "all or none" principle

Striated muscles does not follow "all or none" law

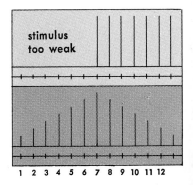

stimulus too weak

1 2 3 4 5 6 7 8 9 10 11 12

BUILT-IN COMMUNICATION SYSTEM

The heart's built-in communication system sets the rhythm of its contractions. It consists of nodal tissue, special conducting tissue found only in the heart. One small bundle of this tissue, forming the sino-auricular (S-A) node, is located in the right auricle, near the large veins. Another patch called the auriculo-ventricular (A-V) node, is embedded in and fused with the tissue in the atrial septum. From here, a bundle of nodal tissue, the A-V bundle, runs downward into the ventricular septum. A branching network of nodal tissue spreads to all parts of the ventricular muscle.

PACEMAKER SYSTEM

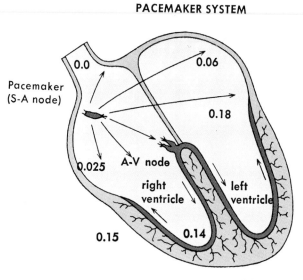

No muscular continuity exists between the atria and the ventricles. Their contraction is transmitted solely by the specialized nodal tissue. The numbers indicate the time necessary for an impulse to travel from the pacemaker to that point, in fractions of a second.

The S-A node is the pacemaker of the heart. Under a given set of conditions, it sets the rate of the heart, which is picked up by all its muscle fibers contracting in unison. In its commanding position, the S-A node determines the rhythm that is picked up by the A-V node. The rhythm then spreads rapidly from atria to ventricles at 16 feet per second. If the S-A node is injured or the heart clamped just below it, the A-V node takes over the S-A node's function, but the heart operates at a lower rhythm. If the A-V node is damaged by disease, a heart block (p. 89) occurs, for, under those conditions, there is no conduction from the atria to the ventricles.

R   L

Photomicrograph of a human A-V bundle (position indicated by arrow). Note the triangular shape of this cross section, with right and left branches originating from its two lower corners. Note how the myofibrils of these specialized muscle cells branch and cross one another at various angles. Base of tricuspid valve is at lower left.

A CONTRACTING MUSCLE GENERATES ELECTRICITY.

Therefore, the heart muscle produces an electric impulse each time it beats. The path of the electrical charge develops first in the atria, then spreads quickly through the ventricles.

During systole, each muscle fiber in the heart behaves like a tiny battery, the current flowing from the active region (negative pole) to the resting region (positive pole). These electrical charges can be recorded by placing electrodes directly on the surface of the heart and connecting them by wires to a galvanometer, an instrument used to measure small amounts of electricity. Obviously, this method cannot be used to record the electrical potential developed by the living human heart.

The beating heart may be regarded as an electric generator that is immersed in a conducting medium. The electric current produced during the cardiac cycle can be "picked up" in the skin. The instrument designed to do this is the electrocardiograph which was invented by Willem Einthoven, the Dutch doctor who also developed the phonocardiograph. The record obtained from the electrocardiograph is called an electrocardiogram (ECG, also EKG).

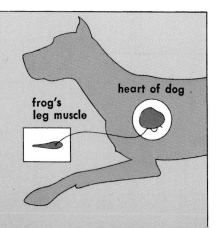

frog's leg muscle

heart of dog

Electric current, in the experiment illustrated here, develops during systole in the heart of a dog and makes a frog's leg muscle twitch. The nerve supplying the frog's leg muscle is placed over the surface of a dog's beating heart. The current stimulates this nerve, which causes the muscle in the frog's leg to twitch in rhythm with the dog's heartbeat.

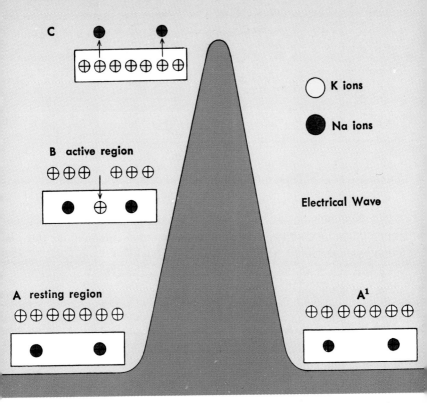

C

K ions

Na ions

B active region

Electrical Wave

A resting region

A¹

ELECTRICAL IMPULSES are generated in the S-A node. These impulses spread over the atrial muscle fibers and the rest of the specialized conducting tissue. Each cell is like a tiny battery with potassium ions (K, yellow) inside, and many more sodium ions (Na, red) outside. The condition at rest is shown in A. When the cell is stimulated, the condition is as shown in B, where the Na ions leak across the cell's membrane. Many others rush in while K ions flow out, as shown in C. This gives rise to an electrical "spark," diagrammed above as a wave. As the current passes on to the next cell, the original condition is restored as shown at position A¹.

THE ELECTROCARDIOGRAPH offers valuable assistance in diagnosis of heart disease. The device picks up the electric impulses produced by the heart during its cycle. In this instrument, invented by Willem Einthoven, a sensitive quartz fiber is suspended vertically between the poles of a strong magnet. This fiber, called the string, is coated with silver or gold; when the impulse is generated, the string is deflected horizontally between the poles. The movements of the string are magnified and projected onto a moving strip of paper. The testing is done with the patient (as illustrated below) lying down, in order to eliminate muscular movement which could interfere with the current recordings; the record of these impulses is called an electrocardiogram (ECG or EKG), revealing the heart's state in health or illness.

Heart waves recorded by the electrocardiograph show the heart's rhythm. Electrodes are placed over the heart, below the left knee, and on both arms below the elbows to pick up these waves.

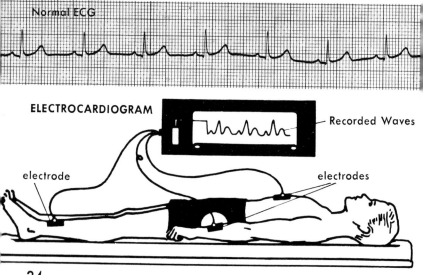

Normal ECG

ELECTROCARDIOGRAM

Recorded Waves

electrode

electrodes

ECG WAVES, known by the letters P, Q, R, S and T, are based on the recordings obtained through positioning of electrodes on the body, with wires hooked to the electrocardiograph. Standard leads include the right and left arm, Lead I; right arm and left leg, Lead II, and left arm and left leg, Lead III. A fourth lead is a chest lead, with one electrode placed on the chest, and another on the left leg. The upward and downward deflections reflect the auricular and ventricular activity of the heart during systole and diastole. The electrocardiograph can aid in diagnosing the injury to a heart muscle caused by coronary occlusion (as illustrated below), or by rheumatic fever, or in evaluating the reaction of the heart to digitalis and other drugs. It can also detect results of mild or so-called "silent" heart attacks.

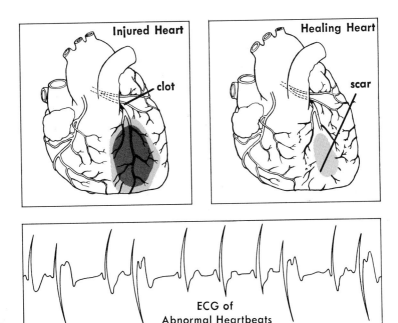

Injured Heart

clot

Healing Heart

scar

ECG of
Abnormal Heartbeats

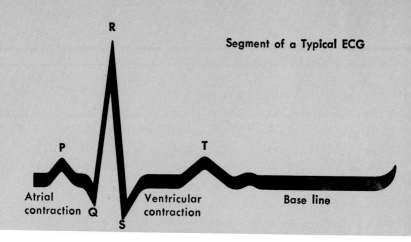

Segment of a Typical ECG

R

P   T

Atrial contraction   Q   Ventricular contraction   Base line

S

A TYPICAL ECG, above, shows the P wave, coinciding with atrial systole, and the QRS wave, marking the ventricular systole. The T wave indicates the end of ventricular systole and the beginning of diastole. The P wave corresponds to the spread of the electrical impulse from the s-a node (p. 30) over the atria and precedes systole by a fraction of a second. The spread of the impulse through the a-v bundle and its branches is recorded as the QRS wave. Ventricular systole begins a fraction

of a second after R, representing the peak voltage. During the T wave the ventricle is relaxing.

An ECG is useful in detecting irregularities in heartbeat, especially those that are due to damage of the heart's conducting tissue. For example, two P waves regularly followed by one QRS wave indicate a 2:1 heart block (p. 89). There are other irregularities, such as atrial fibrillation (uncoordinated and disorganized contraction) and extrasystoles, that are similarly detected in the ECG.

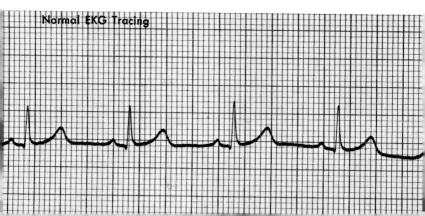

Normal EKG Tracing

TO KEEP THE HEART BEATING requires a properly balanced environment. A mammal's heart, for example, requires a supply of oxygen, a little alkali, and a biological fuel—glucose (a sugar) or lactic acid. In experiments, a frog's heart maintains its normal, automatic rhythmic beat if bathed in a solution containing three kinds of ions (electrically charged particles) in the same concentrations as in the frog's blood. Normally derived from chemicals dissolved in the frog's blood, these ions are sodium, potassium, and calcium. The tracings below illustrate the action of the three ions.

EFFECTS OF CHEMICAL IMBALANCE

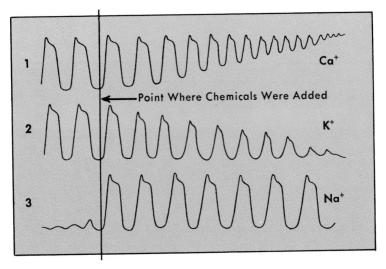

1   Ca⁺

←—Point Where Chemicals Were Added

2   K⁺

3   Na⁺

Figure 1 shows a tracing of the beat of a frog heart in a balanced solution of sodium, potassium, and calcium, indicated by their chemical symbols —Na, K, and Ca. At the arrow, an excess of calcium was added; the heart stopped in systole. In Figure 2, the heart has stopped beating in diastole due to an excess of potassium. In Figure 3, the addition of sodium balances the potassium and restores the beat.

THE WORKING HEART

An athlete or any person who does heavy physical work "is only as good as his heart," people say. They mean that he can do only as well as his heart allows. His performance depends in large measure upon the ability of his heart to supply his muscles with the food and oxygen contained in the blood stream. This ability is governed by (1) the capacity of the heart to pump enough blood to meet the demands of exertion, and (2) the ability of the heart to revert quickly to a resting pulse rate when the exertion ceases.

The heart normally works twice as hard as the arm and leg muscles of a man when running at top speed. Such active muscles approach exhaustion within min-

FOOD AND OXYGEN provide the energy needed to contract the heart muscle. The heart, like other living tissue, derives energy from oxidizing fuels produced by the breakdown of carbohydrates, fats, and proteins in the digestive process. Some of the energy released by this oxidation process is stored in a substance called adenosine triphosphate (ATP).

ATP does not need oxygen to release energy. An electric current generated in each heart cylinder (muscle cell) explodes short bursts of energy through chemical breakdown, not through oxidation.

Oxygen is indispensable to the process of rebuilding ATP so that it can release its energy repeatedly. Oxidation of food is the ultimate source of energy. Although fuel for the heart's energy is drawn from all foodstuffs, at least 35 percent of it comes from the breakdown product called lactic acid. Heart muscle is able to burn up lactic acid as it is formed, but skeletal muscle elsewhere in the body becomes "tired" when its accumulation of lactic acid reaches a critical level.

ANALYSIS OF BLOOD returned to right atrium shows that heart extracts up to four-fifths of the oxygen from blood delivered by coronary circulation. (A heart catheter is used to withdraw a blood sample for this purpose.) Other tissues extract much less oxygen (p. 39). The heart's greater need for oxygen makes coronary circulation more vulnerable to interruption than circulation of blood to the remainder of the body.

utes of exertion. The heart muscle, however, maintains its high energy output continuously without tiring. In extreme exertion, the quantity of blood pumped through the body can be increased to as much as ten times the normal amount. During each minute of exertion, the heart expels four times the total amount of blood in the body.

The heart adapts to the demands of work very quickly, the most rapid acceleration taking place within the first 30 to 40 seconds of increased activity. There is often an increase in the heart rate just before the exertion starts, due to nervous impulses from the cardiac centers in the brain.

Cardiac output (p. 40) is one of the several gauges of the heart's working efficiency.

OXYGEN EXTRACTION FROM BLOOD

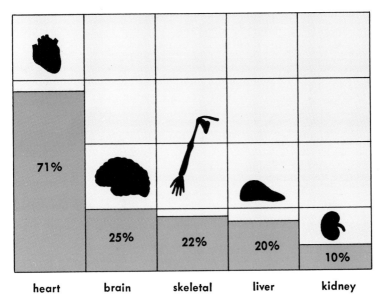

heart	brain	skeletal	liver	kidney
71%	25%	22%	20%	10%

CARDIAC OUTPUT is the quantity of blood that the heart "turns over" in each beat, per minute. Its volume output per beat is called *stroke volume;* the volume output per minute is the *minute volume* and is the stroke volume multiplied by the heart rate.

INDIRECT MEASUREMENT of cardiac output may be accomplished by measuring the quantity of a harmless gas (such as acetylene or ethyliodide) breathed in for one minute. The cardiac output is computed by comparing this amount of gas with the amount absorbed by 1 cc of blood.

In the cardiac output calculated below, the subject has breathed 100 cc of gas in one minute. It is known that 1 cc of blood takes up 0.5 cc of the foreign gas. Therefore, for the blood to have absorbed 100 cc of gas in one minute, 2,000 cc of blood had to pass through the lungs. The amount of blood pumped by one side of the heart is the same as that passed through the lungs during the same minute.

If 2,000 cc is the minute volume and the pulse rate is 70, then the stroke volume is 2,000 cc divided by 70—or 28 cc of blood pumped during each stroke of the heart.

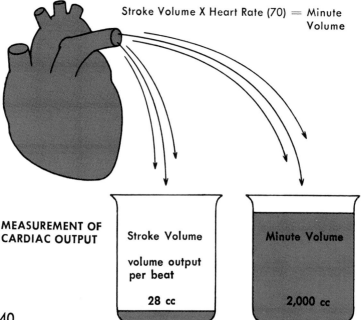

Stroke Volume X Heart Rate (70) = Minute Volume

MEASUREMENT OF CARDIAC OUTPUT

Stroke Volume

volume output per beat

28 cc

Minute Volume

2,000 cc

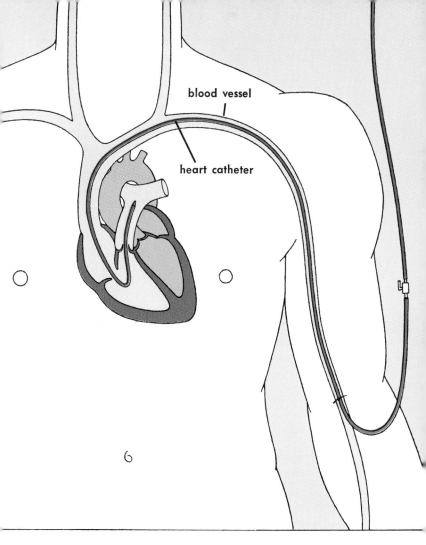

blood vessel

heart catheter

6

THE HEART CATHETER, a device for which Forssmann, Richards, and Cournand received the Nobel Prize in 1956, makes it possible to determine the cardiac output more directly. The catheter, a thin plastic tube, is inserted into a blood vessel or directly into the heart chamber. The blood flowing through the tube is measured electronically. A recording device describes a curve on a moving paper. From this curve, the quantity of blood passing through the heart is measured. The heart catheter is used in research and to diagnose some types of heart disease.

CHANGES IN CARDIAC OUT-PUT depend both on the heart rate and on the blood volume expelled with each beat. Acceleration of the rate increases the number of times the heart expels blood and, therefore, the amount of venous blood returned to be pumped out again. When the beat is so rapid that the filling time (diastole) becomes much shorter, the output from the ventricles is reduced.

At peak exertion, persons in good physical condition may increase their cardiac output from about 2 liters to as much as 35 liters a minute. This is accomplished chiefly by an increase in the stroke volume and to a lesser extent by an increase in the heart rate. Usually, exercises that use most of the body's muscles, such as running or swimming, increase the output more than do "in place" exercises like riding a stationary bicycle. Cardiac output can also be increased by eating and by emotional stress. It is usually decreased by sleep or rest.

The adjustments to pulse rate and to cardiac output are shown in the diagram below.

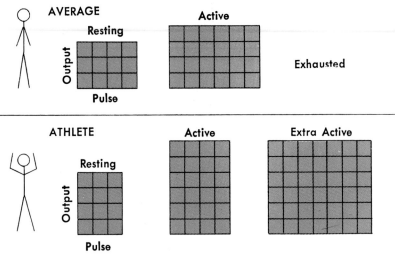

CARDIAC RESERVE is the measure of the heart's adaptability to work. A normal heart responds to the extra needs of activity by increased output with each stroke. If a heart valve fails to close completely, the heart's efficiency is impaired, and the heart beats faster even with slight exertion. But this does not make up for the leakage completely. The person with a leaky valve uses up most of his reserve just to maintain his circulation. His heart is pumping to maximum capacity while he is sitting, and he has no reserve to use when standing. His cardiac output has not increased enough to make the extra effort.

CARDIAC RESERVE

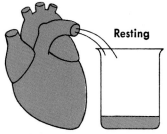

Resting

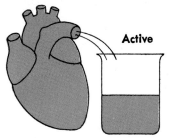

Active

AVERAGE

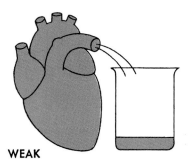

WEAK

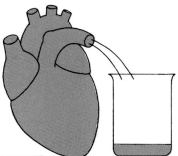

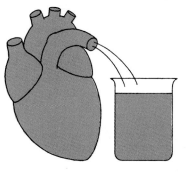

ATHLETE

A heart with a defective valve adapts itself to the body's needs to "compensate" for the leakage. Compensation is partly through increased pulse rate, but more effectively by increasing stroke output. How?

Blood flowing back through the defective valve adds to the residual volume in the ventricles.

This stretches the fibers. The longer the fibers, the more forceful their contraction and the greater the output on the next stroke. Eventually, the muscle enlarges, just as the biceps muscles do from steady, hard work. The ability of the heart to increase its stroke volume, builds up cardiac reserve.

43

THE CARDIAC NERVES

Cardiac nerves control the heart rate in response to the body's needs. During rest, digestion, changes in environmental temperature, muscular work, and emotional excitement or fright, the heart adjusts its rate to the altered demands for oxygen. These adjustments are achieved by the constant discharge of impulses which travel to the heart from centers in the brain along the *efferent* nerves—those going *away from* the central nervous system. The brain centers are influenced by impulses conveyed from various parts of the body such as the stomach, skin, and muscles. These impulses travel along the *afferent* nerves—those going *toward* the central nervous system.

Cardiac nerves are part of the autonomic nervous system, which controls the body functions not under voluntary control. These include, in addition to the heart's rate and force, the movements of the digestive system, secretion of saliva and other digestive juices, and the constriction of blood vessels. The autonomic nervous system has two divisions, the parasympathetic and the sympathetic. Each organ is connected to both.

Two efferent nerves regulate the heart, the vagus (parasympathetic) and the accelerator (sympathetic). The vagus slows down heart action; the accelerator speeds it up. If these nerves are cut, the heart continues to beat rhythmically, but the rate of the beat cannot change.

Afferent nerve fibers—the depressor nerves from the aortic arch and the pressor nerves from the heart's right side—also control heart activity. Both are connected to the medulla, the part of the brain where the cardiac center is located.

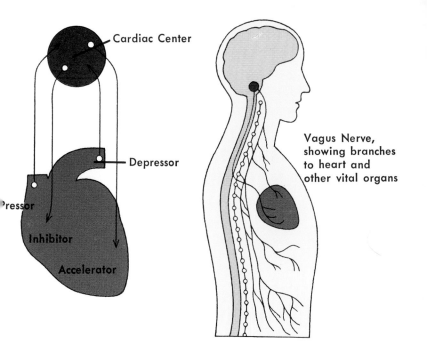

THE VAGUS NERVE starts in the medulla oblongata, just above the spinal cord. The nerve's paired trunks pass downward, one on each side of the neck. The fibers to the heart soon separate from the main trunk; other branches are distributed to the bronchial tubes, lungs, stomach, and intestine. This wide distribution gives the vagus its name, which means "wandering." In the heart, the nerve's fibers end in a ganglion, or clump of nerve cells, in the wall of the right atrium.

When both vagus nerves are cut, the heart beats faster than when they are intact. This indicates that the heart is under constant check by the vagus. It exerts its inhibitory action on the s-a node so that the heart operates as though its brakes were always dragging a little. Reduced activity of the vagus nerve normally results in a mild acceleration of the heartbeat. Continued stimulation may stop the heartbeat, but the heart soon breaks through this inhibition and resumes its beat.

vagus	stimulation	accelerator
Slower Pulse Rate		Faster Pulse Rate

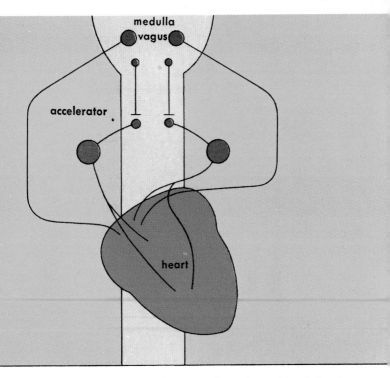

THE ACCELERATOR NERVE fibers originate in the thoracic (chest level) of the spinal cord. These fibers are connected to ganglia in the sympathetic chain that runs alongside the spinal cord. Fibers from this chain then relay impulses to the heart, with fibers terminating in both the atria and the ventricles. Accelerator nerve fibers connect also to the medulla, a bulblike en-

Kymograph Showing Action of Vagus

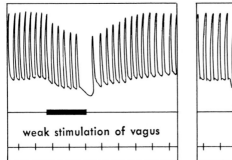

weak stimulation of vagus

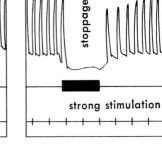

stoppage

strong stimulation

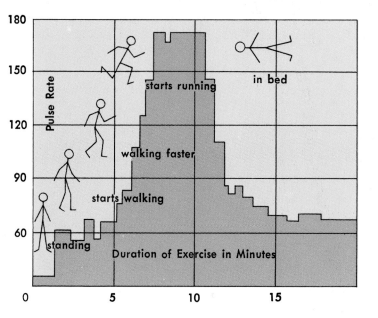

180

150

Pulse Rate

120

90

60

standing

starts walking

walking faster

starts running

in bed

Duration of Exercise in Minutes

0   5   10   15

largement at the upper end of the spinal cord.

Unlike the vagus nerve, which directly controls only the atria, the accelerator nerves increase the rate and force of contraction of both the atria and the ventricles, as well as increasing the a-v conduction. Like the vagus, however, the accelerators exert a continuous effect on the heart. When the sympathetic ganglia are cut, this effect ceases and the heart rate slows down.

The vagus nerve and the accelerator nerves act in harmony, though in opposite ways—one speeding up the heart, the other slowing it down. During physical exercise, for example, the activity of the vagus nerve is reduced, while the activity of the accelerator is increased. Both nerves are constantly active and

the effect on the heart rate is always the result of the actions of both nerves. This dual control permits the most delicate and accurate adjustments of the heart rate and force.

When a man runs, for example, the actively contracting muscles pump blood faster through his veins. Consequently, more blood is returned more rapidly to the right atrium. As the atrium fills and stretches, its wall stimulates afferent nerves that carry impulses to the medulla. In the medulla, the activity of the cardio-inhibitory center is reduced and the cardio-acceleratory center is stimulated, increasing the heart rate. The heart then pumps blood in the greater quantities that a running man's muscles need to continue their activity.

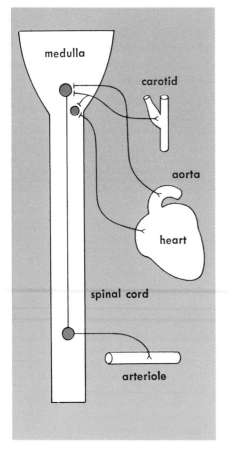

DEPRESSOR AND PRESSOR NERVES in the heart and in the larger blood vessels are even more important than the accelerator nerves in controlling the heart's activity. Nerve endings in the aorta and in its branch, the carotid sinus, are stimulated by a rise in arterial blood pressure. Afferent or *depressor* nerves that carry impulses from the aorta to the cardio-inhibitory center slow the heart by reflex action. Impulses relayed to centers controlling the width of the blood vessels lower the arterial blood pressure.

The large veins in the right side of the heart contain the *pressor* nerves, which ultimately increase arterial blood pressure. These nerves are stimulated when an increased return of blood to the right atrium distends the venae cavae, as during exercise. Impulses carried to the cardio-accelerator center result in a reflex speeding of the heart action, followed by an increase in the arterial blood pressure.

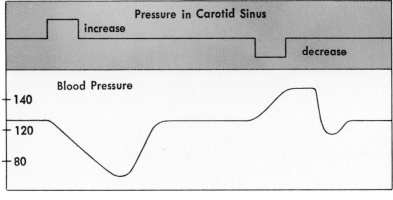

CARDIAC NERVE CENTERS may be influenced remotely. Gentle tapping of the abdominal organs of an anesthetized frog, for example, causes cardiac inhibition. This is shown in the kymographic record here. A sharp blow on the abdominal wall—commonly known as the "solar plexus blow"—will also send sensory nerve impulses to the cardiac centers and cause marked slowing of the heart rate. The inhibition may be great enough to reduce the heart's output of blood and may cause unconsciousness as the brain's blood supply is reduced.

EMOTIONAL STRESS also influences cardiac centers. An athlete before a race, particularly if there is anxiety about the outcome, shows an anticipatory rise in heart rate. Extreme fear, on the other hand, slows the heart rate. In both instances, the impulses come from the higher centers (psychic and emotional) in the brain. Among abnormal conditions which cause an increase in heart rate are hemorrhage, surgical shock, and fever. Tachycardia is a general term meaning increased heart rate; bradycardia means an unusually slow rate of the heart.

Inhalation of irritating vapors, such as ammonia, slow the heart markedly through impulses received from receptors in the nose. Pressure on the eyeballs and stimulation of the equilibrium mechanism in the inner ear also cause the heart to slow down.

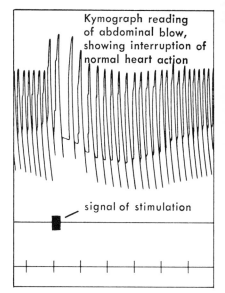

Kymograph reading of abdominal blow, showing interruption of normal heart action

signal of stimulation

OTHER REGULATING CONTROLS include carbon dioxide, which occurs in the tissues as a by-product of food consumption (oxidation) and increases the force and rate of the normal heartbeat.

Adrenalin, a hormone produced by the adrenal glands that straddle the kidneys, stimulates heart action. For this reason, it is sometimes injected to reactivate a heart that has suddenly ceased to beat—as sometimes happens during surgery or to newborn babies. Thyroxin, a hormone produced by the thyroid glands in the neck, also stimulates heart action. These hormones actually speed up the body's metabolism, increasing the output of by-products, such as carbon dioxide, that will also accelerate the heart rate.

THE CIRCULATORY SYSTEM

Blood circulates through a closed system of blood vessels from the heart and back again. To follow the complete circulation route, a drop of blood must travel the pulmonary circulation which carries the blood to the lungs, and also the systemic circulation that supplies all the other organs of the body.

CIRCULATING BLOOD furnishes food and oxygen to the tissues and carries off carbon dioxide and other wastes as they form, and it distributes heat generated by the cells and equalizes body temperature. It also carries hormones made in some organs to be used by others to regulate their special activities, and it conveys antibodies that fight infections and neutralizes some poisons.

To perform these functions and maintain life, the blood must circulate continuously. If the flow of blood to the brain is cut off, consciousness is lost in a few seconds. Within minutes, if the circulation is not restored, the brain cells cease to function permanently. The heart itself cannot survive when deprived of the life-sustaining materials in the blood.

The heart and blood vessels make up the system that circulates the blood, driving it through miles of tubes (arteries, veins, capillaries) in the body.

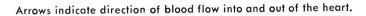

Arrows indicate direction of blood flow into and out of the heart.

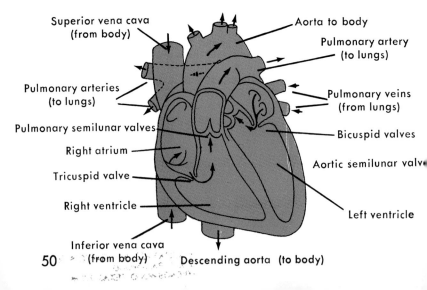

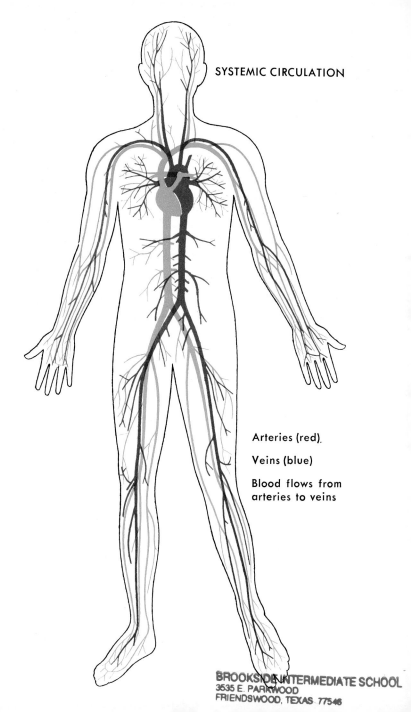

SYSTEMIC CIRCULATION

Arteries (red)

Veins (blue)

Blood flows from
arteries to veins

PULMONARY CIRCULATION aerates the blood in the lungs, supplying it with fresh oxygen and relieving it of some carbon dioxide. The pulmonary circulation begins with the pulmonary artery that carries the venous blood from the right ventricle to the lungs. It ends with the pulmonary veins that carry the oxygenated blood from the lungs back to the heart. Almost immediately after it leaves the heart, the pulmonary artery separates into two branches, one to each lung.

At the lungs, these branches divide into many smaller branches, or arterioles, which reach into every part of the lungs. Each arteriole ends in a **tuft of capillaries.**

A comparable system of branching tubes carries the air that you breath into the lungs. The trachea (windpipe) divides into the two bronchi, and each bronchus divides into numerous smaller tubes. The smallest of these, the bronchioles, ends in the alveoli, which are bunched masses of air sacs.

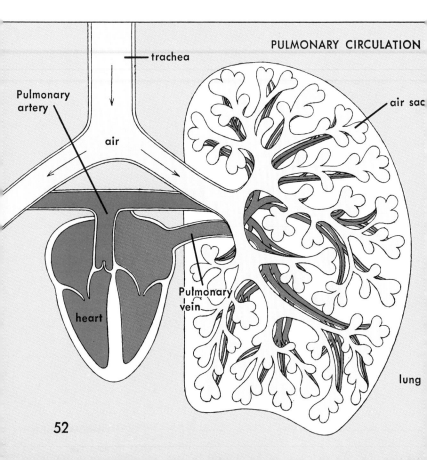

PULMONARY CIRCULATION

trachea

Pulmonary artery

air sac

air

Pulmonary vein

heart

lung

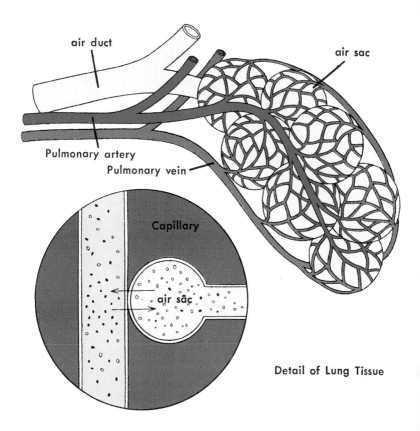

air duct

air sac

Pulmonary artery

Pulmonary vein

Capillary

air sac

Detail of Lung Tissue

EACH AIR SAC, microscopic and numbering into the millions in the lungs, has a wall that is only one cell thick. Bunches of these air sacs are held together by elastic tissue. During inhalation, the lungs are expanded and the air sacs fill with air.

A network of capillaries surrounds the air sacs. Gases can pass easily through the membrane of the thin walls of the air sacs and the capillaries. Venous blood pumped into the lungs from the heart contains more carbon dioxide and less oxygen than the air in the air sacs. An exchange takes place by diffusion through the thin walls of the capillaries and the air sacs. The oxygen content of the blood increases and its carbon dioxide decreases (as it is expelled into the air sacs). In this way, the venous blood is converted into the oxygenated blood that is returned to the left side of the heart and is pumped from the heart through the systemic circulation to all the organs of the body.

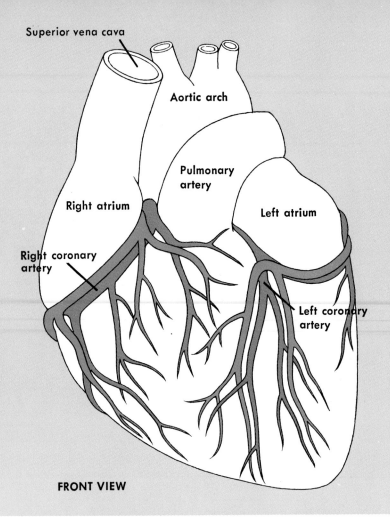

Superior vena cava

Aortic arch

Pulmonary artery

Right atrium

Left atrium

Right coronary artery

Left coronary artery

FRONT VIEW

CORONARY CIRCULATION is a "special" circulatory system that supplies blood to the heart muscle. What makes the coronary circulation special is that the blood flows directly into the right atrium through a vein called the coronary sinus, instead of going through either of the venae cavae.

The coronary arteries, the first branches of the aorta, encircle the heart like a crown. The coronary vessels divide and branch from four main limbs. Every part of the heart muscle, including the septum, receives a rich supply of blood through the fine network of tiny capillaries that surround it.

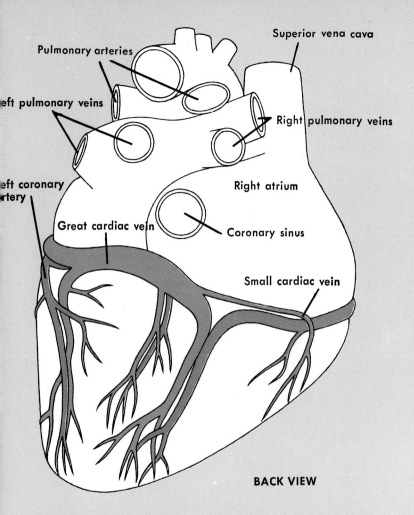

Pulmonary arteries

Superior vena cava

Left pulmonary veins

Right pulmonary veins

Left coronary artery

Right atrium

Great cardiac vein

Coronary sinus

Small cardiac vein

BACK VIEW

A special, lifesaving feature of the coronary arteries is that the smaller vessels from any one of the four main divisions can connect with branches of any one of the other three. This automatically reroutes the blood if a particular branch is blocked by a blood clot. The clogged vessel is thus by-passed, and the starved portion is fed from a new channel. Extra channels that are ordinarily closed also open up and help to redistribute the blood. These interconnections and "spare" blood vessels help to keep the blood in circulation and vital organs functioning after a heart attack.

55

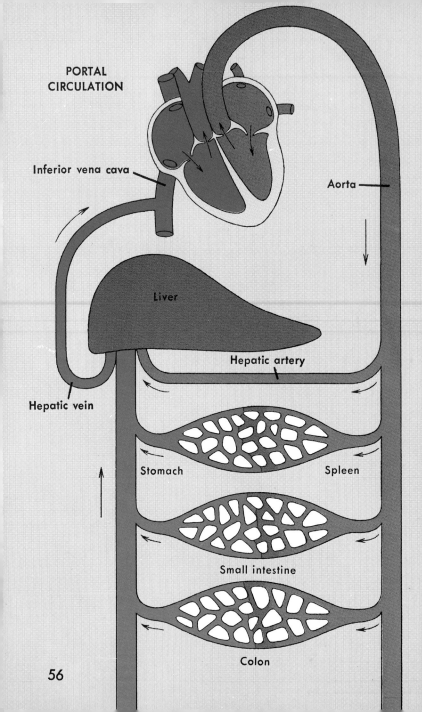

PORTAL
CIRCULATION

Inferior vena cava

Aorta

Liver

Hepatic artery

Hepatic vein

Stomach

Spleen

Small intestine

Colon

56

PORTAL CIRCULATION is "special" because the portal vein is the only vein that empties directly into capillaries. It receives blood from the merging veins of the digestive organs—the stomach, the small and large intestines, the pancreas, and gall bladder—and enters the liver. It carries venous blood, which is rich in digested food and is brought to the liver for further processing before being returned to the heart. The portal circulation furnishes about 80 percent of the liver's total blood supply. The remainder is supplied by the hepatic artery, a branch of the aorta that furnishes the oxygenated blood, which, in turn, nourishes the liver cells.

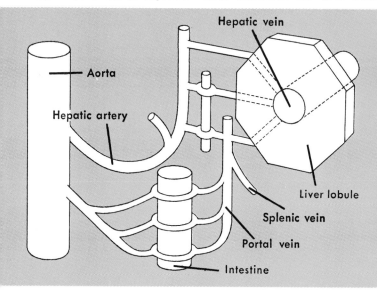

Hepatic vein

Aorta

Hepatic artery

Liver lobule

Splenic vein

Portal vein

Intestine

THE PORTAL VEIN and the hepatic artery each break up into a set of capillaries, so the liver is the only organ that receives both arterial and venous blood.

Branches of the portal vein run between the hexagonal liver lobules, each of which has radiating rows of liver cells surrounding a small central vein. Between the cells are sinusoids, narrow capillary-like spaces. The smallest branches of the portal vein open into these spaces. Capillaries from the hepatic artery also connect with these spaces, and here the mixed blood comes into direct contact with the liver cells.

The sinusoids converge toward the center of the lobule, like the spokes of a wheel, emptying into the central vein. Several such veins merge to form larger veins that finally join to form several hepatic veins that empty into the **inferior vena cava.**

FETAL CIRCULATION feeds an unborn baby in the mother's uterus before either its stomach or lungs are functional. There is no direct connection between the mother's blood stream and that of the fetus, but food and oxygen are filtered through the blood vessels in the umbilical cord and in the placenta, the bag of blood vessels which contains and nourishes the fetus. In the placenta, the capillaries of the mother and the baby come into close contact, and the exchange of food and wastes, and of oxygen and carbon dioxide take place by diffusion.

BEFORE BIRTH, an infant's lungs are small and uninflated. They can accommodate only a small part of the blood from the heart. The remainder flows through two temporary openings: the foramen ovale (a space in the atrial septum) and the ductus arteriosus which joins the pulmonary artery (not yet fully developed) to the aorta. The atrial wall opening is covered by a flap that works like a valve.

THE PLACENTA receives fetal blood from two umbilical arteries, branches of the fetal aorta. Blood is returned to the fetus by a single umbilical vein.

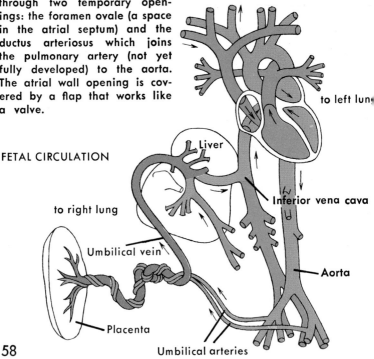

FETAL CIRCULATION

to left lung

to right lung

Liver

Inferior vena cava

Umbilical vein

Aorta

Placenta

Umbilical arteries

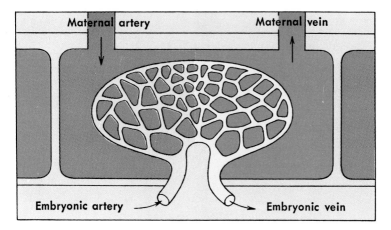

DETAIL OF PLACENTA

THE UMBILICAL VEIN carries blood rich in food and oxygen which mixes with blood of the inferior vena cava, passing into the right atrium. Because the pressure is higher in the right atrium than in the left, the blood pushes aside the valve over the opening in the atrial septum and enters the left atrium, then into the left ventricle from which it is pumped into the aorta.

From the aorta, the blood flows chiefly to the arteries of the heart muscle, head, and forelimbs. The remainder goes to the right ventricle and into the pulmonary artery. Only a fraction of this low-oxygen blood goes to the lungs, however.

About a third of the blood from the aorta passes to the trunk and legs. The remainder goes via the umbilical arteries to the placenta, where it receives more oxygen and food.

AT BIRTH, a number of changes have to take place suddenly so that the baby can live in its new environment. When the umbilical cord has been tied, the infant's source of oxygen is cut off. Carbon dioxide accumulates and stimulates the respiratory center and the baby takes its first breath, inflating the lungs. The lung capillaries widen, accommodating more blood from the pulmonary arteries and less from the ductus arteriosus. Blood returning from the lungs to the left atrium now arrives under higher pressure. The flap over the atrial opening is pushed shut, checking the flow from the right side of the heart.

Eventually, the flap grows into place and the ductus arteriosus closes off. If either of these adaptations does not occur, the heart may become overburdened.

BLOOD VESSELS

The blood vessels are the tubes that carry blood to all parts of the body and back to the heart, delivering oxygen and fuel to the tissues and removing carbon dioxide and other wastes. They are of three kinds: the arteries, the distributing tubes; the capillaries, the immediate supply tubes; and the veins, the collecting or drainage tubes that return the blood to the heart. The arteries branch and become smaller as they reach farther away from the heart. The smallest branches, the arterioles, open into a vast network of microscopic tubes or capillaries, which lead into the venules, the tiny veins that merge to form larger veins.

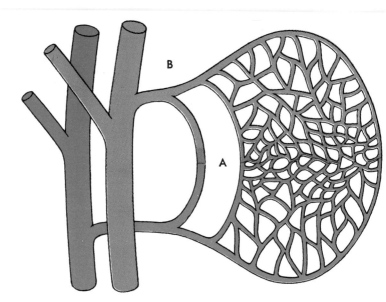

A THOROUGHFARE CHANNEL (A), between the arteriole and the venule, regulates the amount of blood entering the capillary.

A ring of muscle (B) at the entrance to the capillary expands and contracts to allow the blood to pass.

CAPILLARIES, the smallest blood vessels, have a diameter of about 1/2,500 of an inch. This is just wide enough to permit the red blood cells to pass through these vessels in single file. The maze of capillaries is about 60,000 miles in length, or about five yards for every square inch of the body's surface. Their combined diameter is some 600 times greater than the aorta's, which is approximately one inch across.

These microscopic tubes are so widely distributed in the human body that you rarely fail to draw blood from a pin prick anywhere in the skin. The only parts of the body where there are no capillaries are the lens of the eye, cartilage (gristle), and the outer layer of the skin, the epidermis.

Capillary, its wall a single layer of cells thick

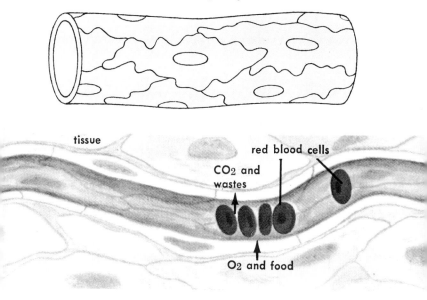

tissue

red blood cells

CO_2 and wastes

O_2 and food

CAPILLARY WALLS are exceedingly thin, being made up of only one layer of flat cells continuous with the cells lining the artery. Through these tissue-thin walls, the exchanges of oxygen for carbon dioxide and of food for waste products take place by diffusion.

Because they are so thin, the capillary walls are not so strong as the arterial walls. If the blood pressure becomes very high, they sometimes rupture. This thinness is, however, an essential property, because it allows fluids to flow through them, supplying food to the tissues.

61

Three Layers of Artery

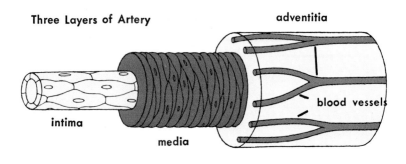

adventitia

intima

media

blood vessels

ARTERIES are thick-walled tubes with three layers. The outer layer, the adventitia, is made of a tough, fibrous supporting tissue that sheaths the artery. In the larger arteries, this layer contains smaller arteries that nourish the arterial wall itself. The middle layer, the media, is composed of smooth (involuntary) muscle fibers and elastic tissue fibers. Both of these fibers run around the artery instead of lengthwise. The inner layer, the intima, consists of flat epithelial cells and elastic fibers. Thin and smooth, this layer offers little friction to the flowing blood.

Like elastic bands, the large arteries stretch as the heart contracts and ejects blood, then recoil as the heart relaxes. In this way, they continue to send blood onward through the arteries even during the heart's resting phase. Small arteries, with predominantly muscle fibers, alter their diameters as they actively contract and relax. They shut down partially when less blood is called for by an organ and open more fully when more blood is needed. Arteries and veins are distinguished from each other by the direction of the flow of blood.

Cross Section of Artery

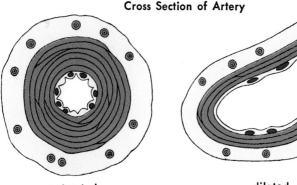

contracted

dilated

VEINS have three-ply walls like the arteries, but the walls are thinner and less elastic. The walls of a vein consist chiefly of muscle and dense fibrous tissue. When it is emptied of blood, a vein collapses; an empty artery remains distended.

Arteries can withstand the high pressure of the blood as it is pumped from the heart. Veins carry blood after it has already passed through the vast network of narrow capillaries, and its pressure has been greatly reduced. A backflow of blood through the veins is prevented by a system of half-moon shaped valves in some veins and by the force of gravity in others.

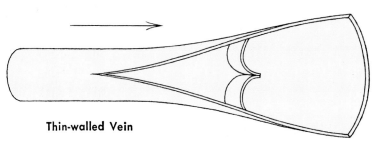

Thin-walled Vein

VALVES IN THE VEINS are arranged in pairs of semicircular pockets, which fill with blood and close the passageway if the blood begins to flow backward —that is, away from the heart. The valves are numerous and closely spaced in the veins of the legs, where the blood must flow "uphill" against the force of gravity. Veins located in the head and the neck, where the blood travels with the force of gravity, do not have valves.

Valves of the Vein

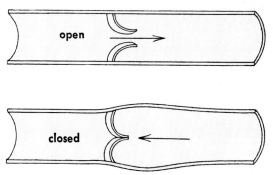

open

closed

REGULATION OF BLOOD-VESSEL SIZE varies the amount of the blood flow in proportion to the needs of the particular parts of the body. When increased activity of any kind makes a demand on the heart for extra blood to supply the necessary energy, the heart responds by increasing its output of blood to all the parts of the body. Since the body's organs are not all equally active at the same time, they do not all need the extra blood, and this puts a wasteful burden on the heart.

The body has a way of ensuring that the extra blood produced by the heart goes only where it is needed. A mechanism in the blood vessels and the nerve centers that regulates the size of the blood vessels makes local shifts of blood from one part of the body to another. Thus, the mechanism copes with the varying demands of the different organs throughout the body. The blood supply can be augmented where it is required at any time of increased activity.

During intense mental effort, for example, the brain requires a larger blood supply than usual, but other parts of the body, such as the skin or the skeletal muscles, do not. A heavy meal requires increased blood flow to the digestive organs, but no more than the usual supply is called for by the brain. These different needs are met by the shifting of blood from one area of the body to another.

By constriction (shown by the partially closed stopcock below) or by dilation (the wide-open stopcock) of specific blood vessels, blood can be shunted to different parts of the body. Where the blood vessels are constricted, less blood is able to flow; where they are dilated, more blood can be moved. The condition illustrated below occurs during muscular activity. During eating, the "stopcock" **action is reversed.**

Schematic diagram illustrates adaptation of blood flow to the rate of tissue activity. Increased stroke and rate of pump increases rate of flow to internal organs and muscles. Stopcocks would serve to shunt blood to different regions at different rates.

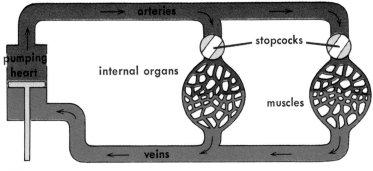

VASOMOTOR NERVES, distributed to the smooth muscle in the walls of the larger blood vessels, control the diameter of the vessels and, hence, the volume of blood transported. Most blood vessels have only vasoconstrictor nerves, which cause the muscle to contract and reduce the size of the vessel.

Blood vessels in the salivary glands, muscles, reproductive organs, and digestive system have both vasoconstrictor and vasodilator nerves. Through constriction and dilation, blood can be shunted from one region of the body to another.

During vigorous exercise, inhibition of vasoconstrictors and stimulation of vasodilators causes arterioles in the muscles to be widely dilated. At the same time, blood vessels in the stomach, intestines, spleen, and kidneys are constricted. The blood shift is chiefly to the muscles and brain. As body heat rises, more blood is shifted to the skin, and heat is conducted away from the body.

Vasomotor nerves, like the cardiac nerves, are regulated through reflex centers. The vasoconstrictor center is in the medulla; the vasodilator centers are located at several different levels of the spinal cord. The constrictor influence is the greater, and the vast bed of small arteries is generally in a state of partial constriction. If the spinal cord were cut at B, control from the vasomotor center would fail, and blood vessels would dilate; cuts at A and C would have little effect on vasoconstrictor center.

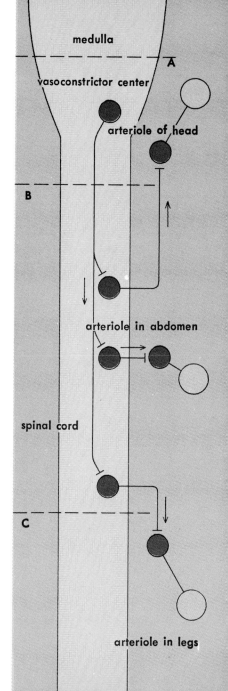

medulla

A

vasoconstrictor center

arteriole of head

B

arteriole in abdomen

spinal cord

C

arteriole in legs

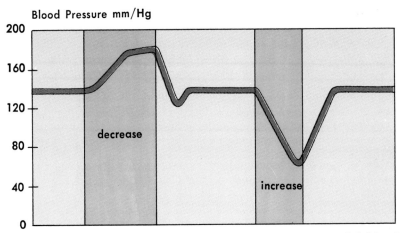

Blood Pressure mm/Hg

decrease

increase

The kymograph record above shows the effect on arterial blood pressure of decreasing (left) and increasing (right) the pressure within the carotid sinus (branch of the aorta).

VASOMOTOR CENTERS receive as well as discharge impulses. The depressor nerve (p. 48) in the aorta's walls not only reduces heart action but also inhibits the vasoconstrictor center. Thus, fewer impulses are discharged to the blood vessels, and blood pressure is reduced.

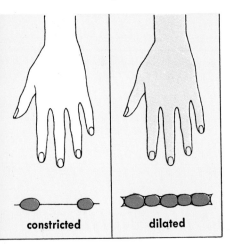

constricted   dilated

Meals, external temperature, muscular activity, change in posture, and emotions are among the conditions that affect the vasomotor centers. When you stand up suddenly, the blood vessels in your legs and abdominal organs are promptly constricted, shunting blood to your head. If this adjustment fails to take place, dizziness or even fainting is likely to occur.

A sudden blast of cold air does not shut down the blood vessels in your skin directly. Rather, impulses from the skin nerve endings are conveyed by afferent nerves to the vasoconstrictor center, and then a volley of impulses is promptly discharged to the blood vessels. The blood vessels constrict, and the skin pales. By the same mechanism, the skin reddens with warmth, because its blood vessels are dilated as a result of reflex action.

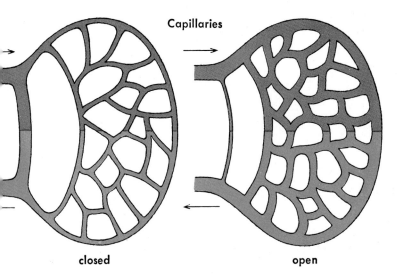

Capillaries

closed   open

VEINS AND CAPILLARIES are supplied also with vasomotor nerves. More than either arteries and veins, the capillaries are subject to changes from completely closed during rest to wide open during vigorous activity. In active muscles, this effect is produced by the combined action of chemicals and nerves. Carbon dioxide and lactic acid are formed in greater amounts by active muscles and cause dilation of the capillaries.

Capillaries permeate every tissue of the body except the epidermis, the cartilage, and the cornea and lens. No cell is ever more than 5/1000 of an inch from a capillary. The ready exchange of food and wastes within the body is made possible by the thinness (less than 1/10,000 of an inch) and permeability of the capillary wall.

It has been estimated that if the capillaries were laid end to end, the total length would be nearly 60,000 miles and their total bulk would be more than twice that of the liver, the body's largest organ. If all of the capillaries were open at the same time, the blood would be pooled from the entire body, leading to a drop in blood pressure incompatible with life. However, by constriction and dilation, the blood can be shifted from an inactive organ to active tissue.

Other substances that affect capillary size are the hormones adrenalin and corticosteroids released from the adrenal glands. They cause the capillaries to constrict. Acetylcholine liberated at nerve endings causes capillaries to relax. In conditions of shock, extensive tissue injury, and acute infections, substances are released that may cause such widespread dilation of the capillaries as to result in the collapse of circulation.

BLOOD SUPPLY to heart muscle is governed by the caliber of the coronary arteries and their branches. These vessels receive fibers from both the vagus and the sympathetic accelerator nerves. The heart's blood vessels, like others in the body, either open fully or constrict, depending upon the workload. The vagus causes vasoconstriction; the sympathetic causes vasodilation. Stimulation of the sympathetic may double the flow of blood into the coronary arteries.

In a dog, experimental stimulation of the stump of a severed vagus reduced the coronary flow when the heart rate was maintained constant. When the vagus is intact, it is constantly active in varying degrees, slackening its effect during increased activity and increasing during rest. It slows the heartbeat at the same time it constricts the coronary arteries. The accelerator is active only during vigorous exercise.

SENSITIVITY TO OXYGEN is also unique in coronary circulation. Chemical dilators—lactic acid, epinephrine (also called adrenalin), and acetylcholine—act either directly on the arteriolar wall or through the nerves that are distributed to it. They help to restore coronary circulation and replenish the heart's oxygen supply. An inadequate supply of oxygen causes severe chest pains, an ailment called angina pectoris.

DURING SYSTOLE, the coronary blood vessels are compressed by the heart's contraction and the blood flow is reduced. The heart muscle, therefore, loses color and blanches.

DURING DIASTOLE, its color returns, for unlike the rest of the body (excepting the muscles), the heart's blood vessels receive their greatest blood flow during diastole.

Color Changes in Heart

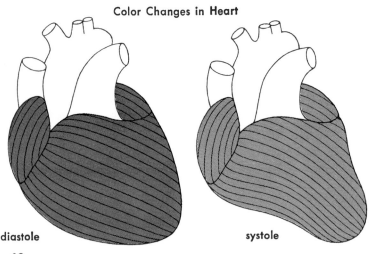

diastole   systole

Results of experiment to determine rate of blood flow at different levels of activity

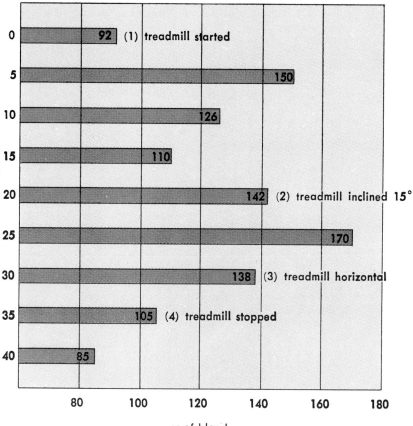

	cc of blood
0	92 (1) treadmill started
5	150
10	126
15	110
20	142 (2) treadmill inclined 15°
25	170
30	138 (3) treadmill horizontal
35	105 (4) treadmill stopped
40	85

cc of blood

A FLOWMETER was inserted into the coronary artery of a dog in order to measure the blood flow during exercise on a treadmill. At (1), the treadmill was started; at (2), it was inclined at a 15° uphill gradient; at (3), it was horizontal; and at (4), the treadmill was stopped.

The results of this experiment indicated that the blood flow was greatest during the work peak and least when the activity had stopped.

BLOOD TRAVELS AT VARYING SPEEDS along the vascular system. It moves swiftly through the large arteries, then more slowly through the arterial branches. Its speed drops sharply in the capillaries, then increases again in the veins. In the great veins, blood travels at a rate near that in the aorta.

Blood, like flowing water, adjusts its speed to the cross section of the channel, or bed, in which it is flowing. As the aorta branches into arteries, and the arteries into arterioles and finally capillaries, the total cross section of the blood stream increases, and the speed of the blood is progressively reduced. As the blood returns to the heart, along the smaller and larger veins, the cross section of its bed is reduced, and its speed increases. The capillary bed cross section is about 600 times greater than that of the aorta, whose diameter is approximately one inch. The blood, therefore, flows 600 times slower.

The mean blood flow in the aorta is about 12 inches per second and only slightly less than that in the larger arteries. In the capillaries, it is about one-sixtieth of an inch per second; in the large veins, about 8 inches per second.

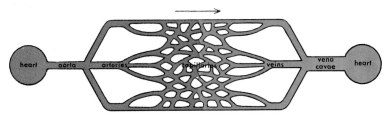

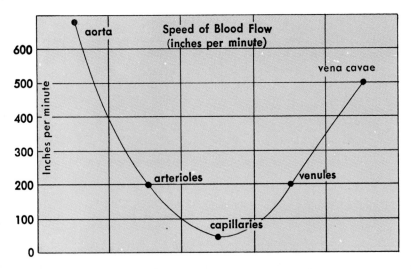

CAPILLARY FLOW differs not only in its slow-crawl rate but also in the way the blood flows. In the large arteries, the flow pulses, coinciding with the pumping and resting of the heart. When an artery is cut, the blood has a spurting flow. In the capillaries, however, the flow is a steady one. Blood flows smoothly from cut veins as well as from cut capillaries.

Large arterioles can stretch; the small arterioles, due to their narrow bore, resist being stretched. When a large artery stretches, only a portion of its blood passes onward during systole. The remainder is squeezed onward during diastole, when the elastic arterial wall recoils. Thus, the pulsing blood flow evens out in the capillaries. The constancy and slowness of flow allow for the exchange of materials between the blood and the tissues. The steady flow of blood also prevents bursting of the thin walls of the capillaries under high pressure.

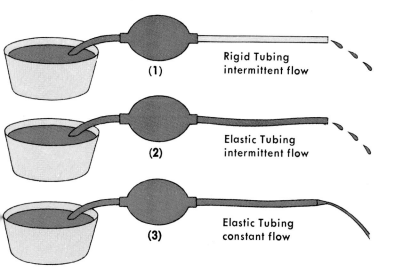

(1) Rigid Tubing intermittent flow

(2) Elastic Tubing intermittent flow

(3) Elastic Tubing constant flow

DIFFERENCES IN TUBE STRUCTURE have an effect on the flow of a liquid through them, as shown in the experiment illustrated above. In a system with a rigid tube of uniform diameter, the flow is intermittent, coinciding with squeezing or "pumping" the syringe (1). The same pulsing flow occurs in a system with an elastic tube of uniform diameter (2). With a combination of an elastic tube, corresponding to the elastic arteries, and a tapering nipple, corresponding to resistance in the arterioles and capillaries, the flow is constant (3).

CIRCULATION TIME is the time it takes for a drop of blood to make a complete circuit through the body, returning to the spot where it started. This, of course, is determined by the particular path it takes.

A complete circulation from the left ventricle through the coronary vessels to the right side of the heart, and then through the pulmonary circulation and back to the left ventricle requires much less time than a circulation to the toes and back. If the blood passes through the stomach or intestine, it has to travel through three sets of capillaries rather than the usual two, the time will be even longer. Average circulation time is 24 seconds. The journey through the coronary circulation is about 16 seconds; through the portal circulation, about 30 seconds.

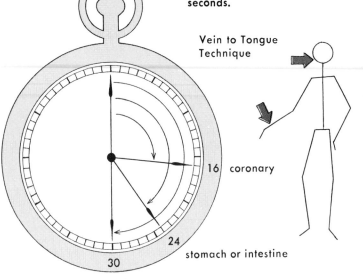

Vein to Tongue Technique

16 coronary

24

30

portal

stomach or intestine

MEASUREMENT OF CIRCULATION time can be made in several ways. One method used in man is the "vein to tongue" technique. A sweet- or bitter-tasting chemical is injected into an arm vein. The substance is pumped by the heart to the arteries and finally to the capillaries in the tongue, and the subject indicates to a technician holding a stopwatch the moment he tastes the chemical. This circulation time has been measured as 13 seconds. More complicated methods include the injection of dyes or radioactive substances, whose progress as it flows through the vessels is recorded with instruments.

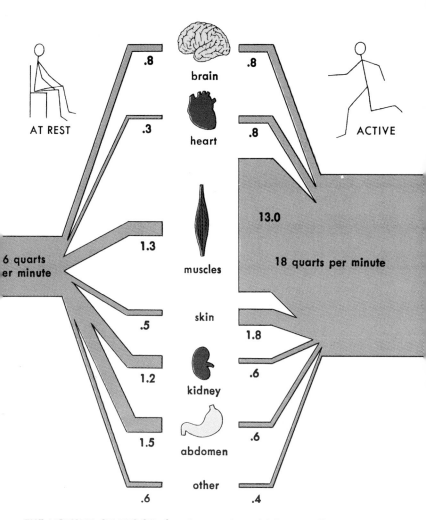

AT REST

6 quarts
per minute

brain .8
heart .3
muscles 1.3
skin .5
kidney 1.2
abdomen 1.5
other .6

ACTIVE

18 quarts per minute
13.0

brain .8
heart .8
muscles
skin 1.8
kidney .6
abdomen .6
other .4

THE VOLUME OF BLOOD that is delivered to an organ depends on the number of blood vessels it contains. This means that the brain receives at least ten times more blood per unit of weight per minute than do the skeletal muscles. In other organs, such as the spleen and muscles, the amount of blood delivered varies widely at different times. Capillaries that are closed during rest open during activity. In this way, the blood vessels serve as a reservoir from which blood may be shunted from one region to another by the mechanism of constriction and dilation of the blood vessels described earlier (pp. 64 and 65).

BLOOD PRESSURE

Blood is forced through the arteries under tremendous pressure. When a large artery is cut accidentally, the blood spurts several feet. This pressure, generated by the heart and the muscular contractions in the arteries, is measured in millimeters of mercury (mm Hg), the figures representing the height that a column of mercury would be pushed up by the pressure of the blood at the point in the circulatory system where it is measured.

In the aorta, the blood pressure may average 130 mm Hg; in the large arteries (such as the brachial artery in the arm), 110; and in the smaller arterioles and capillaries, to 5 or 10 in the veins, and to less

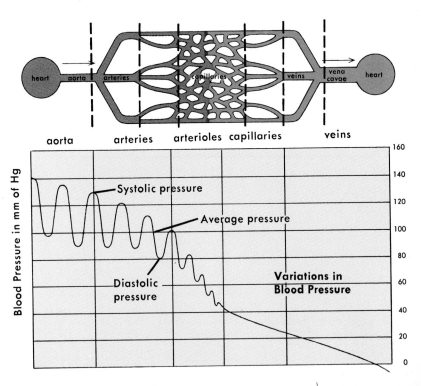

than zero (in relation to atmospheric pressure) in the largest veins.

Blood pressure varies also with the heart's systole and diastole. The ejection of the blood during systole causes a sudden rise in arterial pressure. In diastole, pressure immediately falls as the arteries push the blood onward. Blood pressure is, therefore, recorded in two figures, typically 120/80 or 150/70. The first, the systolic pressure, denotes the pressure in the arteries during systole and indicates roughly the force of the heartbeat. The second, diastolic pressure, denotes the pressure during diastole and indicates chiefly the muscle tone of the smaller arteries. Together, the systolic and diastolic pressures reflect the condition of the circulatory system.

PULSE PRESSURE, the arithmetical difference between systolic and diastolic pressures, is the effective force that keeps the blood flowing. If the systolic pressure is 120 and the diastolic pressure 80, the pulse pressure is 40 mm Hg. If either the systolic pressure is low or the diastolic high, the pulse (effective) pressure is insufficient. Both are significant in interpreting the pressure factors of the system.

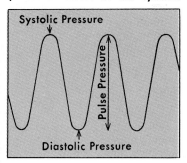

Systolic Pressure

Pulse Pressure

Diastolic Pressure

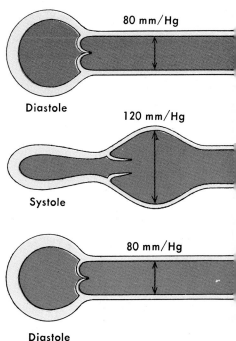

80 mm/Hg

Diastole

120 mm/Hg

Systole

80 mm/Hg

Diastole

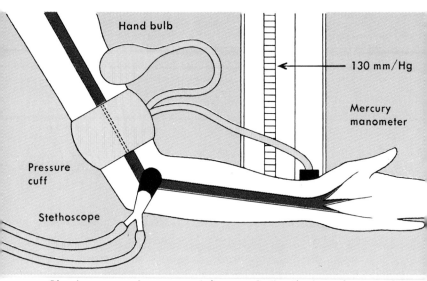

Blood pressure is measured in man indirectly by using a sphygmomanometer (*sphygmos*, from the Greek, meaning "pulse"; manometer, meaning "pressure measurer"). A direct measurement could be made by inserting a tube into the artery.

A SPHYGMOMANOMETER consists of a rubber cuff, an air-compression bulb, and a graded glass tube containing mercury (the manometer). The rubber tubes connect the cuff with the manometer and with the hand bulb. The cuff is strapped firmly around the upper arm, and air is then forced into the cuff by pumping the compressor bulb.

This shuts off the artery in the arm, allowing no blood to flow through. At the same time, the column of mercury rises in the manometer to, say, 130 or over.

The air is then slowly released by opening the pin valve in the bulb, and the pressure in the cuff falls to the point where the force of the blood just overcomes the pres-

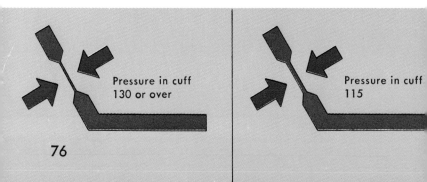

Pressure in cuff 130 or over

Pressure in cuff 115

sure in the cuff. The reading of the manometer represents systolic pressure. During diastole, the artery snaps shut because the cuff pressure is still higher than in the artery. The sudden closing of the artery during each diastole produces a sound heard through a stethoscope placed in the crook of the arm. The air is permitted to escape slowly from the cuff until the sound just disappears; then the diastolic pressure is read.

NORMAL BLOOD PRESSURE in healthy persons varies with age, body position (sitting, lying, or standing), time of day, emotions, meals, external temperature, and, most of all, activity. Up to middle age, men normally have a somewhat higher blood pressure than women. In both sexes, blood pressure rises moderately with age, the systolic more than the diastolic. However, there is no fixed formula, such as "100 plus your age" to determine correct blood pressure.

Systolic pressure in adults generally ranges between 100 and 150, diastolic between 70 and 95. Prompt adjustments in blood pressure are necessary to meet changing conditions. If you feel dizzy when you jump out of bed in the morning, your vasomotor system may not be adjusting the blood-vessel size quickly enough. This is known as "poor vascular tone" but does **not in itself indicate illness.**

BLOOD PRESSURE is generally lower during rest or sleep, when you are lying down. It is higher in the evening than in the morning, and it may rise when you are angry or excited. It is lower when you are frightened, when the weather is hot, or after a warm bath. Blood pressure rises after a heavy meal, when you are cold, or after fast walking, running, climbing stairs, or riding a bicycle, when **extra blood is needed.** In the physically fit, these adjustments are made promptly and with a minimum increase in heart rate.

Astronauts experience rapid changes—from one G (gravity on earth) to 6 or 8 G's at blastoff and then zero G during weightlessness. In the course of training in centrifuges and other devices simulating these exposures in pressure chambers, the astronaut "trains" his vasomotor centers to make the necessary **adjustments in space flight.**

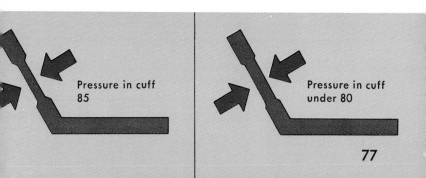

Pressure in cuff
85

Pressure in cuff
under 80

DEFECTIVE, DAMAGED OR DISEASED

Coronary disease may occur in any of the many parts of the heart or in any of the blood vessels of the circulatory system, including the large arteries and the arterioles. It can also affect the kidneys, adrenals, thyroid, or the nervous system.

The underlying cause of heart diseases may be a birth defect or childhood infection. In later life, an early weakness may be aggravated by emotional tension, physical overwork, cigarette smoking, or use of drugs. Diabetes, overactive thyroid, adrenal-gland tumors, emphysema, asthma, or a kidney ailment are among the diseases that may impair heart function. Wherever the trouble starts, the heart is ultimately affected because the workings of these organs are interrelated, sometimes through feedback mechanisms.

One of the most common disorders, hypertensive heart disease, begins in the arterioles. In a person whose blood pressure has been consistently high, the heart must pump with increased force against a high resistance to the blood flow. This extra work enlarges the heart muscle (a condition called hypertrophy), which further raises the arterial blood pressure and eventually damages the blood vessel walls, placing a still greater load on the heart and gradually reducing its efficiency. The overworked system works poorly and delivers less oxygen. Oxygen insufficiency can cause damage to the kidney and the brain as well as to the heart itself. When the blood vessels in the kidney are thickened or are otherwise damaged, these organs release substances that raise the blood pressure still further, and as a result, the cycle of cardiovascular-renal (heart-kidney) disease develops.

UNDERLYING CAUSES OF HEART DISEASE

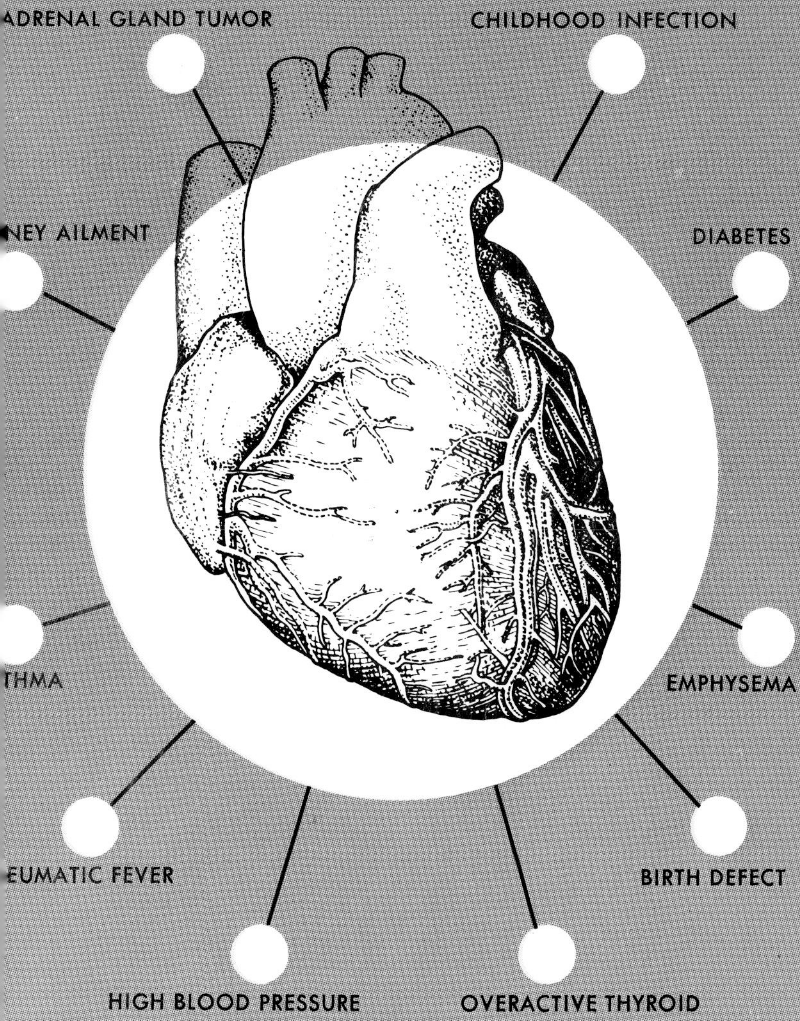

ADRENAL GLAND TUMOR

CHILDHOOD INFECTION

NEY AILMENT

DIABETES

THMA

EMPHYSEMA

EUMATIC FEVER

BIRTH DEFECT

HIGH BLOOD PRESSURE

OVERACTIVE THYROID

79

HYPERTENSION, or high blood pressure, is common in almost a third of all heart ailments and is a first sign of possible trouble. Symptoms do not always exist. When they do, headaches, dizziness, fatigue, flushing, and general aches and pains occur. These are warning signals, calling for a visit to the doctor.

ESSENTIAL HYPERTENSION is a term derived from the theory that high blood pressure may be an "essential" part of a person's makeup or a family trait, as his body build or his personality. It usually develops in persons whose parents (either or both) suffered from hypertension. When both parents are normal, the chance of offspring developing hypertension is only 3 out of 100. The primary mechanical difficulty is excessive resistance to the blood flow in the small arteries which increases diastolic pressure.

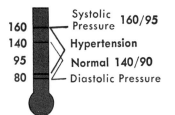

Date	Blood Pressure
sitting	164/98
standing	176/110
pulse	78

As advanced medical knowledge disclosed some of the factors that cause high blood pressure, some cases once thought to be essential hypertension are now classified as "nonessential," or traceable hypertension. The causes of essential hypertension are unknown and difficult to treat.

Major factors causing traceable hypertensions are: (1) faulty nervous control of the arterioles, (2) kidney disease, (3) disturbances in adrenal glands, and (4) structural changes in the large arteries.

BLOOD-PRESSURE READINGS from "normal" to "high" can be seen in the diagram. Doctors are more concerned about the *diastolic* pressure because it represents the constant force exerted on the arteries without the added pressure of the heart's contraction during systole. Patients usually quote the higher, or systolic, reading.

Even "normal" blood pressure fluctuates widely. Anxiety before a physical examination may cause it to rise. A doctor may ask his patient to rest before he takes several readings in both sitting and standing positions.

EXCESSIVE NARROWING of the arterioles checks the flow of blood into the capillaries, raising diastolic pressure. This may be due to an increased flow of nerve impulses along vasoconstrictor nerves, an exaggerated sensitivity of the nerve endings in the walls of the blood vessels, or a failure of afferent nerve endings to signal stretch forces. These points in the reflex arc are shown in the diagram. Normally, a rise in arterial blood pressure initiates a reflex that slows the action of the heart and lowers blood pressure by depressor nerves (p. 48).

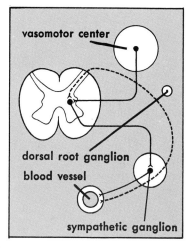

Blood pressure rises in persons "keyed up" with fear, joy, anger, or worry because messages from higher nerve centers constrict the arterioles.

Excitable persons are believed to be more sensitive also to circulating chemicals in the blood that "tighten up" the small blood vessels. These chem- icals (hormones) come from the medulla and cortex of the adrenal glands. The medulla produces epinephrine (adrenalin) and norepinephrine, which, in excess, causes diastolic pressure to rise. A hypertensive person is up to ten times more sensitive to the blood-pressure-elevating effect of norepinephrine.

Measurement of blood pressure is simple, reliable, and painless, giving clues to condition of heart and blood vessels.

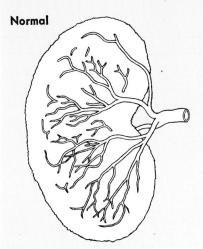

Normal

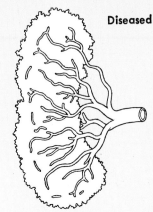

Diseased

SOME KIDNEY DISEASES produce hypertension. Bright's disease (chronic inflammation of the kidneys' filtering cells) and a narrowing or blocking of the renal arteries are common causes. The damaged kidney releases renin, a substance that, in turn, releases angiotensin, a substance that raises the blood pressure. Angiotensin may cause a direct narrowing of the arterioles, or it may stimulate the vasoconstrictor nerves. It also may bring about an increased production of the hormone aldosterone (p. 83). Angiotensin has been used to raise blood pressure in persons who are in shock after surgery.

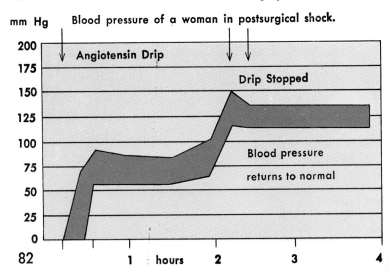

Blood pressure of a woman in postsurgical shock.

82

ADRENAL GLAND disturbances also produce hypertension. One of the few curable causes of hypertension is pheochromocytoma (dark-colored tumor) that occurs on the medulla of the adrenal gland. It causes an outpouring of a mixture of two hormones, epinephrine and norepinephrine. One way of diagnosing the existence of the tumor is by chemical tests of the urine in which a by-product of the damaging hormones can be detected. If it is not recognized early, pheochromocytoma may prove fatal. If detected in the early stage, the tumor can be removed, and the patient is spared damaging complications.

Aldosterone, a hormone produced by the adrenal cortex, prevents the elimination of excessive salt and water in the

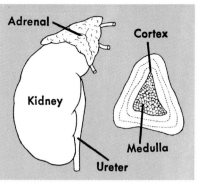

kidney, a condition which, in turn, raises blood pressure. The hormone returns to the bloodstream much of the sodium the kidneys filter out. The excess salt holds back water in which it is dissolved. This increases the volume of blood and raises the pressure. It is possible, too, that sodium ions also increase the heart's contractile force.

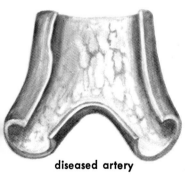

diseased artery

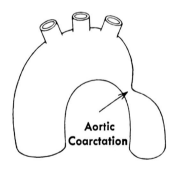

STRUCTURAL ALTERATIONS in the large blood vessels may increase systolic pressure mechanically. For example, a sudden narrowing of the aorta (aortic coarctation) as it descends into the abdomen acts as a "roadblock" to the blood flow in the smaller vessels. More often, a

loss of elasticity in the large arteries reduces their ability to accommodate blood discharged during systole. This is caused by a thickening and hardening of the arterial wall, called atherosclerosis (p. 84). The diagrams show a diseased artery and coarctation of the aorta.

ATHEROSCLEROSIS, a form of hardening of the arteries, causes most heart attacks. It may also cause "strokes" and gangrene of the legs. Derived from the Greek words *athere* (gruel or mush) and *skleros* (hard), the name describes the injury to the arterial wall. The deposit of fatty material in the lining layer in major arteries is at first soft or mushy. Gradually hardening, it becomes a plaque. As more plaques form and "age," the arterial wall thickens and the channel narrows. In advanced cases, the channel is nearly closed. Pieces of the plaques that break off and travel with the bloodstream may plug up a small artery, just as lime coats and finally clogs a water pipe. Circulation is impaired.

A FULLY DEVELOPED PLAQUE contains fatty acids, lipoproteins (proteins with fat components), calcium salts, cholesterol (a waxy substance normally found in blood and tissues), scar tissue, and threads resembling *fibrin*, a product formed in normal clotting. An early lesion shows up as fatty streaks on the artery lining that may become a point of occlusion.

Photograph at left shows a normal coronary artery in cross section; at right, atherosclerotic deposits have formed on artery's inner lining, reducing its capacity for carrying blood.

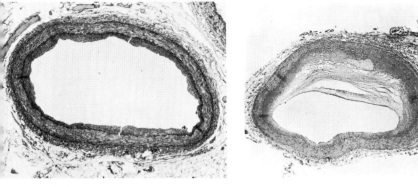

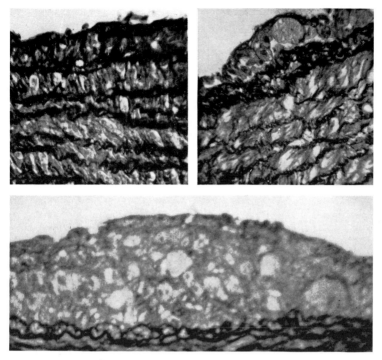

(Upper left) Normal section of arterial wall; (upper right) a few foam cells penetrate the endothelium; (bottom) micrograph shows a larger accumulation of fat deposits.

EVOLUTION OF THE PLAQUE may start in one of several ways. Experiments with animals have shown that fat molecules may enter the arterial wall by moving between the cells of the lining or by large foam cells carrying them through. Smaller fat molecules become trapped and accumulate in the arterial wall. The force of the blood against the walls contributes to the process of plaque accumulation. Therefore, when blood pressure is high, the condition is compounded.

In susceptible persons, the arteries may actually pick up fat from the circulating food supply. In patches of normal and atherosclerosed arteries grown in test tubes, the diseased tissue absorbed more fat but failed to break it down.

Another theory is that plaque formation begins after an injury to an artery's inner wall. A clot may form on the lining surface, perhaps accelerated by a tendency to abnormal clotting. Substances from the blood may then build up around it.

Healthy artery (left), thrombus in large artery (center); thrombus loose in artery (right).

A THROMBUS is a local clotting of the bloodstream. A dangerous condition exists when a thrombus clogs the blood vessel, a condition referred to as thrombosis. This is one of the effects of atherosclerosis. Enzymes in the arterial wall break down the fatty materials, releasing fatty acids and cholesterol—crucial irritants that inflame, ulcerate, scar, and roughen the normally smooth arterial lining. This further impedes the flow of blood through the already narrowed opening, leading to clot formation and further complications.

A blood clot may form in any part of the body, but clots are more likely to form in certain areas. Both atherosclerosis and thrombosis usually begin at points where the artery forks, or curves, or is otherwise subject to added resistance or strain. Particularly vulnerable areas are the coronary arteries, the aorta, and the arteries in the neck and brain, where the full impact of the heart's pumping action is received. Also vulnerable are the branches of the abdominal aorta where they split to form the large arteries supplying the lower extremities.

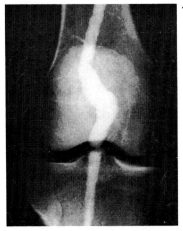

◄**AN ANEURYSM** is a pocket or "balloon" in an artery wall that has been weakened by atherosclerosis. This condition commonly occurs in the aorta where it passes into the abdomen. Pressure of an aneurysm on neighboring organs interferes with their functioning and causes severe pain. A greater danger of existing aneurysm is the possible rupture of the artery, which produces a massive hemorrhage and subsequent death. The X-ray picture shown here reveals an aneurysm in a leg artery.

A CORONARY HEART ATTACK begins with the vulnerable coronary arteries, particularly where the blood vessels bend into the muscle. The squeezing action with each systole increases the pressure on the vessels' walls at these points. (This has been compared to stepping on a garden hose when the water is turned on full.) The narrowing of the coronary arteries, especially when complicated by atherosclerosis, may partially or completely shut off the blood supply to a portion of the heart muscle.

The effect may be: (1) angina pectoris (pain in the chest; irregular or weakened heartbeat); (2) myocardial infarction (destruction of part of the heart wall); or (3) sudden death from complete failure of the heart if a clot, or thrombus, becomes lodged in a major branch. When a small branch is blocked, the portion of the heart muscle formerly supplied by this artery dies. Scar tissue forms over the damaged area when such an injury (infarct) heals.

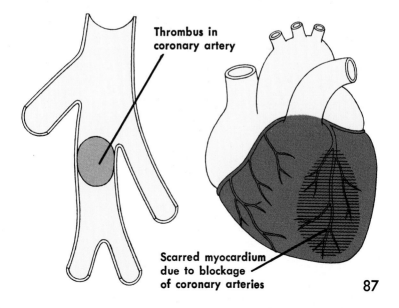

Thrombus in coronary artery

Scarred myocardium due to blockage of coronary arteries

87

ANGINA PECTORIS—literally "strangulation of the chest"—is a pain or pressure signaling that the heart is not getting enough oxygen. The heart pumps harder to drive blood through the stiffened arteries and its demand for oxygen increases. The narrowed coronary arteries diminish the oxygen supply and local anemia causes the severe pain.

Distribution of anginal pains through the body

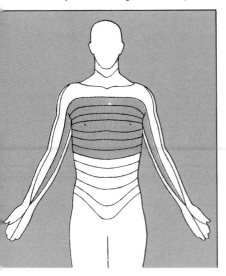

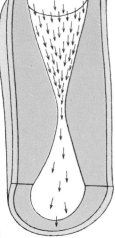

ANGINAL ATTACKS are often brought on by physical exertion (particularly after meals), by exposure to cold, emotional disturbance, or excitement.

Some victims describe angina as a heavy weight pressing on the chest. Others say it is "like being crushed between two trucks," or a burning feeling under the breastbone, or a choking sensation. The discomfort spreads to the arms (usually the left), neck, jaw, and back. Angina, mild or severe, may occur for the first time after recovery from a heart attack. In some persons, however, the first heart attack occurs after many years of angina attacks. In others, death has occurred during angina pectoris.

Nitroglycerine tablets placed under the tongue relieve anginal spells, usually within minutes. The drug, believed to dilate the blood vessels, temporarily increases the local blood supply. To prevent an anginal attack, the heart's collateral circulation (p. 54), the enlargement of some arterial branches, and the opening of new ones help the patient.

◄ In a heart that has suffered an attack, the coronary artery and its branches are narrowed to such an extent that normal flow of blood is diminished.

IRREGULAR HEART RHYTHM may also signal the slow "rusting" process in the coronary arteries. The significantly arrhythmic heart may skip beats or beat wildly. The rhythm may be very rapid or may be less than 40 beats per minute. Irregularities are usually traced through an electrocardiogram (ECG), a record which measures the electrical impulses in the heart and shows any deviation from a healthy pattern. The ECG may show that damage to the heart has occurred without the person knowing it—in a "silent" heart attack—or it may point to an acute coronary insufficiency, causing persistent pain and fainting spells. The cause in both cases is blockage of a small artery, insufficient oxygen, and some localized damage to the heart muscle.

CONGESTIVE HEART FAILURE results from diffuse weakening of heart muscle by continued inadequate blood supply. The fluoroscope (a kind of X-ray machine) may show an enlarged heart shadow with the walls thinner than normal. The initial sign could be shortness of breath. Later, inefficient pumping results in edema: water accumulation in the lungs, abdomen, and legs, especially around the ankles. The added weight of the retained water increases the work load of a weakened heart.

To rid the body of excess fluid, diuretics are given to promote urine excretion. To reduce the accumulation of water, salt intake is restricted. These measures do not repair the damage but the process may be arrested by medical treatment.

IN A PARTIAL HEART BLOCK, one of every two, three, or four impulses gets through. The result is a 2:1, 3:1, or 4:1 atrioventricular rhythm. In a total block, the atria and ventricles beat independently, the ventricular beat being much slower. Today, it is possible to restore the heart's normal rhythm by use of an artificial pacemaker, an instrument which generates a current that stimulates the heart (p. 139).

Heart blocks may be produced in an animal by putting a clamp on its heart at the atrio-ventricular junction. This interference with conduction produces varying degrees of heart block.

Normal 1:1 Rhythm

Block 2:1 Rhythm

Complete Block

Tune Record in Fifths of Second

THE CORONARY-PRONE are persons most vulnerable to coronary heart disease. What are the features that help to identify a likely candidate for a heart attack years before the first signs of coronary disease appear? To identify these features, scientists use epidemiologic studies which examine and statistically relate certain factors in a human population. Factors in those who succumb are compared with those who remain free from attack.

A famous epidemiologic study was started in the early 1950's on 5,000 men and women in Framingham, Massachusetts. The characteristics of people who developed coronary disease were compared with those of people who did not during the years of observation.

This study showed that those who developed coronary heart disease had the following characteristics: (1) high serum cholesterol, (2) high blood pressure, (3) overweight, (4) emotional stress, (5) physical inactivity, (6) overdevelopment of left ventricular muscle with abnormalities in the ECG, (7) a history of heart attacks in the family, and (8) heavy cigarette smoking. Not all eight characteristics were present in all coronary victims, but those who remained free of the disease lacked these characteristics.

In a study that will ultimately include 100,000 people, the U.S. Public Health Service puts high serum cholesterol, high blood pressure, and cigarette smoking as the "three worst suspects."

MAJOR CAUSES OF CORONARY HEART DISEASE

Serum Cholesterol Levels (mg%)
Expected rate of CHD
200: 46%
200-219: 60%
220-239: 81%
240-259: 139%
240-259: 194%
260+

Blood Pressure (mm/Hg)
120: 36%
120-139: 92%
140-159: 98%
160-179: 160%
180+: 227%

Smoking
Expected rate of CHD
nonsmokers: 60%
smoking: 126%

Combination of Factors
Expected rate of CHD
none: 45%
any one alone: 117%
any two together: 213%
all three: 563%

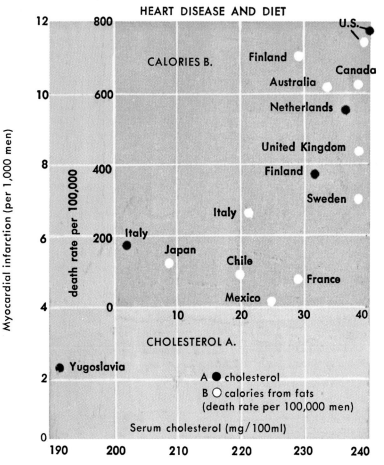

HEART DISEASE AND DIET

Myocardial infarction (per 1,000 men)

death rate per 100,000

CALORIES B.

U.S.
Finland
Canada
Australia
Netherlands
United Kingdom
Finland
Sweden
Italy
Italy
Japan
Chile
France
Mexico

CHOLESTEROL A.

Yugoslavia

A ● cholesterol
B ○ calories from fats
(death rate per 100,000 men)

Serum cholesterol (mg/100ml)

CHOLESTEROL in the blood was found to be related to heart attacks in a study by a team of scientists at the University of Minnesota. This conclusion was arrived at by determining the average amount of cholesterol in the blood of the male populations in different countries. The cholesterol level was highest in the United States, where the number of heart attacks also rates the highest. Yugoslavia and Japan are low in both. The study indicates that cholesterol levels may be related to the different eating habits of these populations.

COMPARING CHOLESTEROL AND BLOOD PRESSURE from a study made in Westchester, New York, blood pressure ranked as the more important cause of coronary disease. The statistical risk of a coronary mounts with the number of characteristics occuring together in one individual. Of 6,000 men aged 36 to 50 in the Westchester study, those with both high blood pressure and high cholesterol had a heart disease rate more than four times greater than men with low blood pressure and low cholesterol. The most vulnerable—the man with a "coronary profile"—is pictured as middle-aged, obese, hypertensive, and having high serum cholesterol. He is physically inactive, ambitious, aggressive, subject to emotional stresses, and a heavy smoker.

THE "HEALTHY" CHOLESTEROL level in the bloodstream has not been clearly established.

The presence of cholesterol in atherosclerotic plaques and in the blood in high quantities of persons with coronary disease has made this fatlike, waxy substance a prime suspect. Direct evidence that it is a cause has not yet been found. The "circumstantial evidence" is based on experiments with animals made atherosclerotic artificially and on observations of humans, normal and diseased.

Cholesterol is measured in milligrams percent (mg%), or per one hundred milliliters of serum (1/5 of a pint). A milligram is 1/1000 gram; a gram, 1/28 of an ounce.

In the United States, a cholesterol level of 260 mg% is high; 200 mg% or less, low.

HIGH FAT, HIGH CHOLESTEROL diets have produced atherosclerotic plaques in experiments with rats, rabbits, chickens, pigs, dogs, and monkeys. Before the plaques appear, the blood becomes "flooded" with cholesterol. A change of diet can halt or reverse this buildup.

Both animals that eat animal fat (e.g., dogs, whales) and others that do not (e.g., pigeons) develop atherosclerosis naturally.

Rabbit given estrogen and cholesterol (left) has almost no atherosclerosis in aorta; rabbit that got only cholesterol (right) has heavy atherosclerosis.

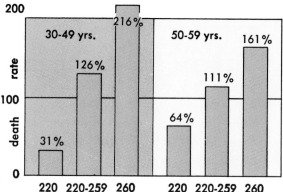

Framingham Study Group of coronary heart disease risk in men ages 30-59

30-49 yrs.   50-59 yrs.

216%   161%
126%   111%
31%   64%

rate   death

cholesterol level   220 220-259 260   220 220-259 260

OBSERVATIONS ON HUMAN BEINGS suffering from diseases in which the cholesterol levels are high (diabetes and nephrosis, a kidney disease) show that they tend to develop atherosclerosis. Persons with malnutrition from wasting diseases, such as cancer and tuberculosis, have both low cholesterol levels and less tendency to coronary disease. A study of ulcer patients in England and the U.S. showed that those on a milk-cream diet had coronaries at a rate twice as great as those not on the diet.

The greatest accumulation of evidence that high cholesterol levels are significant in coronary attacks comes from population studies in such cities as Los Angeles, Chicago, and Albany. In the Framingham study, men in the group with less than 200 mg% of serum cholesterol developed coronary disease less than half as frequently as the total population. In the group with cholesterol levels of 260 mg%, the rate was almost twice that of the total population.

While atherosclerosis cannot be linked solely to cholesterol, a high level of cholesterol increases the risk of heart disease. Other factors being equal, the lower the serum cholesterol, the lower the coronary risk.

Framingham Study Group of coronary heart diseases.

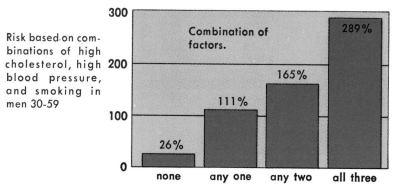

Risk based on combinations of high cholesterol, high blood pressure, and smoking in men 30-59

Combination of factors.

289%
165%
111%
26%

none   any one   any two   all three

A FOCUS ON FAT began when scientists discovered that the liver manufactured cholesterol no matter how little fat was eaten, thus maintaining a high cholesterol level in the blood. Further, it was noted that Eskimos, who are high-fat consumers, were rated low in coronary proneness. For these reasons, attention was then focused not only on the amount but also on the type of fat consumed.

FATS, or lipids, include triglycerides, cholesterol, phospholipids (fats linked to organic phosphorus), and lipoproteins. Triglycerides may be saturated, monounsaturated, or polyunsaturated, the fatty acids in all three consisting of a long chain of carbon atoms each attached to two hydrogen atoms. A saturated fat contains all the hydrogen it can hold. The monounsaturated fat can link up with two additional hydrogen atoms. The polyunsaturated fat can link up with four or more.

Saturated, or "hard," fats are generally, but not always, animal fats, and they usually solidify at room temperature. Polyunsaturated fats are found mostly in vegetable and fish oils, and they remain liquid at room temperature.

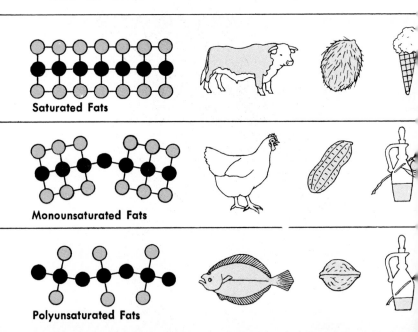

Saturated Fats

Monounsaturated Fats

Polyunsaturated Fats

THE "PRUDENT DIET" of the Anticoronary Club added a significant link in the chain of suspicion that fats are related to atherosclerotic heart disease. This experiment, conducted by the Bureau of Nutrition of New York City's Department of Health, was begun in 1957 when volunteers, men aged 40-59, went on "prudent diets" of low calories and low fat (about twice as much polyunsaturated as saturated).

RESULTS of the experiments, which lasted over four years, showed that the blood cholesterol level of the dieters dropped from 260 to 230 within the first year. In a control group of nondieters, the cholesterol level remained about the same. The higher the prediet level, the greater the fall in cholesterol. Experimenters analyzed a tiny amount of fat removed from under the skin of the dieters to determine whether they were staying on their diets. More polyunsaturated fat was deposited in their fatty tissues than in the nondieters.

A comparison of attacks after four years revealed a rate of 339 attacks per 100,000 in Anticoronary Club members; 980 per 100,000 in the controls..

Despite these results, scientists feel they have not proved conclusively that a diet which lowers the blood cholesterol also decreases heart attack risk. Further studies are needed with more people over a longer period of time and with tighter controls. A ten-year study is being conducted by the U.S. Public Health Service.

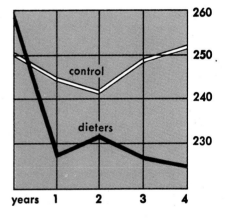

Effect of "prudent diet" on cholesterol in the blood.

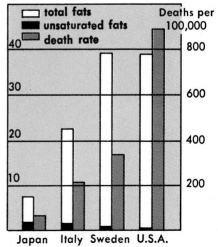

% total dieters

AGE AND SEX as risk factors have also been studied. Records show that a majority of the American soldiers killed in the Korean War had narrowing of the arteries, 22 years being the average age of the soldiers. Today, many men between the ages of 45 and 55 have heart attacks, some fatal. "Rusting" of the arteries is a long-term process. The earlier the process starts, the greater the risk of an "early" attack. Atherosclerosis is not a disease strictly of old age, as once believed. Nor is it inevitable with aging. Some men of 80 and 90 are remarkably free of atherosclerosis.

During middle age, the death rate from heart attack is about five times higher in men than in women, as shown in the chart of a study of men and women aged 45 to 54. Estrogen, the female hormone, is the

Coronary deaths Sex and Risk (rate per 100,000 population) 45-55 years	
	white male 348.4
white female 65.9	

factor believed to protect women. After menopause, the risk in women rises as the estrogen supply declines. By age 75, the rate for women approaches that of men. Injection of estrogen in humans lowers the cholesterol levels. In rabbits and male chicks on high cholesterol diets, atherosclerosis was checked by female hormone injections. Arteries of those not given hormones were obviously more narrowed (p. 92).

OVERWEIGHT is not in itself a cause of heart disease. Excessive pounds do, however, increase the risk of hypertension, higher blood-cholesterol level, and diabetes, and indirectly increases its probability.

Excess weight reduces lung capacity and available oxygen, and this adds to the heart's workload. Fatty tissue may penetrate the pericardial sac and even the heart muscle. Diabetes, definitely aggravated by obesity, is a factor in heart disease because it may cause damage to the arteries.

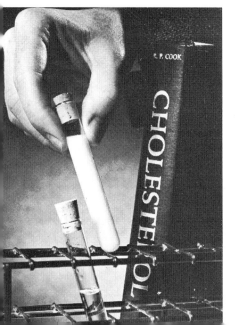

Blood serum is normally clear but turns milky when cholesterol is high.

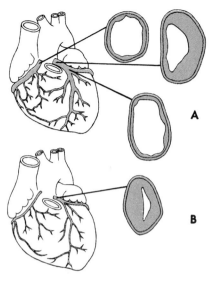

Differences in atherosclerotic narrowing of blood vessels in a physically active person (A) and a sedentary person (B).

A

B

PHYSICAL INACTIVITY, with no regular exercise, may be a risk factor. Dr. Paul Dudley White, the eminent heart specialist, said, "Hard work never hurt a healthy human heart." Physically active men are less subject to heart attacks, or they are more likely to survive attacks and will recover more rapidly than inactive men.

Among possible explanations, vigorous activity seems to favor development of collateral circulation (p. 55), enlarging and strengthening heart muscles. Cholesterol and triglyceride levels in the blood are reduced, speeding up removal of serum fat and keeping down body fat.

Physical exertion stimulates the thyroid gland, accelerating the rate at which fats are "burned up." It also increases lung capacity and oxygen supply. Body stress brings on an increased adrenalin secretion, releasing more fat into the bloodstream. But physical activity raises the body's resistance to stress conditions.

SMOKING has not been linked directly to coronary disease, but statistics show that the death rate from heart disease is much higher among cigarette smokers than nonsmokers. Autopsy examinations of heavy smokers shows marked thickening of the walls of the bronchial tubes and the arterioles, reducing their diameters, clogging and rupturing air sacs, and destroying their capillaries. This reduces the total oxygen supply. Inhalation of smoke increases the heart's workload and reduces the oxygen available to the muscle. The nicotine in tobacco stimulates the adrenal glands to produce hormones which release more fatty acids into the bloodstream.

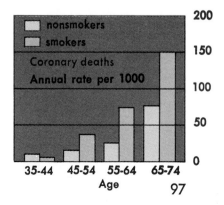

nonsmokers
smokers

Coronary deaths
Annual rate per 1000

200
150
100
50
0

35-44   45-54   55-64   65-74
Age

97

STROKES, like heart attacks, are the climax of a progressive narrowing and blocking of the blood channels by atherosclerosis. When the blood supply to parts of the brain is cut off or reduced to a trickle, a stroke occurs, and the nerve cells in that area cease to function. The result may be paralysis or loss of speech, vision, or memory. Strokes are a hazard to young men and women as well as to older people.

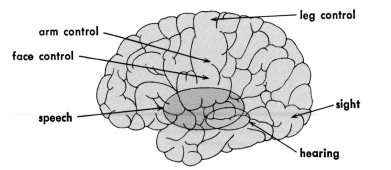

Halt of blood flow to control zones of brain (arrows) affects speech, hearing, sight and arm and leg control.

CLOGGING of a cerebral artery or neck feeding blood to the brain (Fig. A) is the most common cause of a stroke. A cerebral thrombus is a clot in a brain artery damaged by atherosclerosis. A cerebral embolus usually lodges in a brain or neck artery.

A diseased vessel, or aneurysm (p. 86), can burst and flood brain tissue (Fig. B). Such a hemorrhage is more likely when atherosclerosis and hypertension exist. Compression of an artery by accumulated blood and displaced brain tissue (Fig. C) can also cause a stroke.

Clotting   Hemorrhage   Compression

A   B   C

NO SINGLE ARTERIAL BRANCH supplies any particular part of the brain. An intricate network of alternate routes permits redirection of the blood, thus allowing recovery of some or all brain function. If this occurs, paralyzed muscles may recover strength, lost speech may return, and impaired memory may be restored.

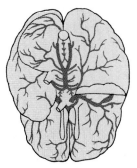

REHABILITATION after a stroke calls for massage and manipulation of the muscles to prevent crippling deformities. Until the patient is able to do the proper exercises without assistance, a nurse must move his limbs for him. Return to normal activity depends to a great extent on the patient's perseverance and will to recover.

Self-help, using a variety of devices, is part of rehabilitation therapy. The U.S. Public Health Service booklet, *Strike Back at Stroke,* and the American Heart Association's *Do It Yourself Again* give directions for restoring use of muscles.

Not all strokes cause massive damage. Many people suffer "little strokes"—temporary attacks due to insufficient blood and oxygen in the brain. Warning signals, all due to atherosclerosis, vary: sensations of fleeting numbness and weakness in one side of the face, in the arm, leg, hands, or fingers; momentary blackouts and blurred vision; head noises; a sense of confusion; slurred speech; faulty memory. These "little strokes" may lead to mental deterioration, emotional derangement, and childish, confused, senile behavior.

New methods of treatment may avert serious strokes. High blood pressure can be controlled by drugs and a tendency to clot formation reduced by anticoagulants. Plugs are removed from arteries by surgery; artificial tubes used to replace diseased portions. Aneurysms are removed; vessel walls mended with plastic patches.

Rehabilitating stroke patient to use of arms

ANGINA IN THE LEGS (medically, thromboangiitis obliterans) is due to poor circulation, a result of atherosclerosis of the leg arteries. Among the signs are pain and cramps in the calf muscles, causing lameness in walking; numbness in the legs, feet, or toes; and sudden blanching of the legs when elevated or turning blue in a standing position. Sensitivity to cold may also increase, and slow-healing ulcers form on the feet and toes.

More men than women suffer from this kind of angina. When the pain comes in spells, aggravated by walking and relieved by rest, the condition is called intermittent claudication.

Treatment can relieve the pain and halt the advance of the disease. Anticoagulants are used to check blood clotting, and enzymes are used to dissolve clots which have formed in the leg arteries. Clots can also be removed by surgery.

A change of diet, both to lose excess weight and to slow the process of atherosclerosis, may be advised. Specific remedial exercises promote collateral circulation and improve nourishment to leg arteries.

Gradations of hypertension as it affects the eye

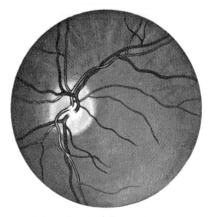

Sclerosis of retina—mild narrowing of arteries

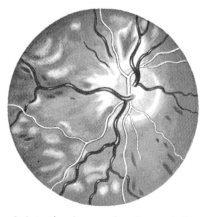

Sclerotic hemorrhaging and edema of retina

DIABETES, a metabolic disease, causes damage to the smaller arteries, especially in the legs, feet, and eyes. In the legs, it may cause gangrene, which sometimes requires amputation.

In the eyes, it may cause hemorrhage of the retina, edema, and blindness. Today, diabetes can be controlled by the intake of insulin and other drugs so that **it does not reach this stage.**

VARICOSE VEINS are stretched or diseased veins, primarily in the legs. They occur especially in people whose jobs require long periods of standing. They can also be caused by garters or other tight clothing that restrict circulation. Extra pressure on the valves damages the tissue and still further impedes the return of venous blood to the heart. Varicose veins sometimes occur during pregnancy. A tendency toward weak veins or valves may be inherited.

Soreness, fatigue, and cramps in leg muscles and itching and swelling around the ankles are among the symptoms. Skin discoloration and leg ulcers may result if condition is neglected.

Treatment may involve injecting glucose into affected sections of the veins, tying off, surgical removal, or rerouting of vein strips. Walking and swimming stimulate circulation in the defective veins. Wearing elastic stockings, using bandages, elevating the legs from time to time, and shifting positions all help to restore circulation.

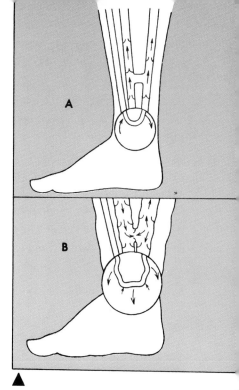

▲

(A) Normal leg, with intact veins and valves, and normal venous return. (B) Leg with varicose veins, diseased and stretched, that result in stagnation of blood, discoloration, and edema.

LOW BLOOD PRESSURE or hypotension—indicated by a systolic reading of 100 mm Hg or less—often follows extensive blood loss, chronic severe anemia, or other debilitating diseases or infections. As with hypertension, hypotension is called "essential" when it is not related to any known cause. People with low blood pressure, generally free from physical symptoms or even discomfort other than tiredness and faintness, have a longer life expectancy than those with high or even normal blood pressure.

If low blood pressure is due to anemia or a chronic infection, it will return to normal when the cause is removed. If caused by loss of blood through accidental hemorrhage or surgery, blood volume is restored by the body itself or by a blood transfusion. Corrective drugs include norepinephrine, which raises blood pressure.

INFECTIONS that do not attack the heart directly but occur elsewhere in the body may lead to heart damage. Attacks of rheumatic fever, scarlet fever, syphilis, or tuberculosis may also cause heart ailments. Control of infections by vaccines and antibacterial drugs has eliminated heart disease from some of these causes, but rheumatic heart disease, the only preventable major heart disease, still causes more long-term disabling illness in children than any other illness. Rheumatic fever, a streptococcal infection, occurs most often in children between 5 and 15, usually developing after a "strep" sore throat.

RHEUMATIC FEVER ATTACKS often recur, and they are believed to produce an allergic reaction that ultimately damages the heart muscle. Sometimes all three layers of the heart wall become inflamed. As in any scarring process, the inflamed area is invaded by blood cells, fibrin and platelets from clotted blood, and embryonic connective-tissue cells.

Sometimes healing is complete. However, if the disease continues and involves the myocardium, it may eventually lead to cardiac failure. In a long-diseased heart, when there has been acute rheumatic heart disease in childhood, the heart muscle fibers disintegrate. When the valves are also affected, the sick heart cannot take on the added burden.

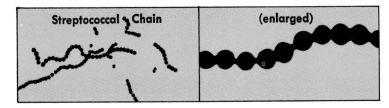

Streptococcal Chain   (enlarged)

DIAGNOSIS OF A STREP INFECTION is confirmed by finding an organism called Group A beta-hemolytic streptococcus in a throat culture. Antibiotics, particularly penicillin, are given for about ten days to eliminate the bacteria. Symptoms are a fever of about 101, a sudden sore throat with painful swallowing and swollen glands, and nausea or vomiting. These danger signals call for immediate medical attention.

VALVES DAMAGED BY DISEASE interfere with the normal one-way flow of blood. Blood leaks back into the atria or the ventricles through valves that no longer close tightly, causing the heart sounds known as "murmurs." The heart then resembles a worn-out, leaky pump. But just as a leaky pump can draw enough water if the handle is worked harder, so the heart has a built-in mechanism which compensates for defective valves by pumping more vigorously to deliver an adequate amount of blood. There are several causes of valve deformities, but the commonest by far is rheumatic fever.

LEAKY SEMILUNAR VALVES allow blood to flow back into the left ventricle as the elastic wall of the aorta recoils. This blood has to be pumped out again by the now relaxed ventricle on the following beat. Improperly functioning a-v valves force the atrium to contract more often and vigorously to compensate for the backflow that occurs as the ventricle contracts.

STENOSED VALVES, believed to be the result of an allergic reaction to repeated attacks of rheumatic fever, become scarred or roughened and have a buttonhole-like appearance, the result of a progressive healing of damaged tissue. The openings of the valves are narrowed or "stenosed" by this scarring process adding a burden to a heart with leaky valves.

stenosis of mitral
and tricuspid valves

aortic stenosis

CONTROL OF STREPTOCOCCAL INFECTIONS is the key to prevention of rheumatic fever and, in turn, of permanent heart disease. A child who has had one attack must be guarded against repetition, since each recurrence increases the likelihood of further damage to the heart. People with a history of rheumatic fever may contract the disease again at any age, though the risk decreases as they grow older.

BACTERIAL ENDOCARDITIS is an infection that results in inflammation of the heart's lining. Patients with rheumatic heart disease are especially vulnerable so they are given heavy doses of penicillin as preventive treatment. Surgery that is normally only a minor hazard may be dangerous for people with a history of rheumatic fever. Ordinarily harmless bacteria may produce infection in already-damaged valves. Penicillin is, therefore, given one or two days before an operation.

Bacterial endocarditis may be acute or subacute, but both forms are extremely serious. They follow streptococcal or other bacteriological infections occurring elsewhere in the body. The acute form may cause ulcerative destruction of a heart valve and is often rapidly fatal, the subacute form being commonly less deadly. Penicillin, which may control the bacterial infection, has no effect on heart damage that may already exist. Predisposing factors are prior injury and congenital defect.

Bacterial Endocarditis

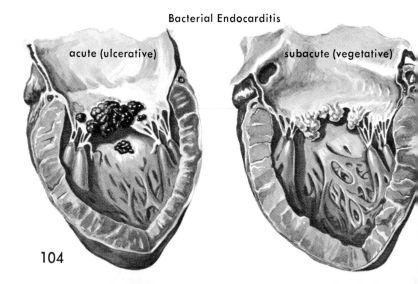

acute (ulcerative)

subacute (vegetative)

ABOUT ONE IN EVERY THREE ▶ children attacked by rheumatic fever for the first time is left with heart damage. Continuous treatment is necessary to prevent a recurrence. A special type of penicillin that is released slowly from the muscle is injected monthly. Less expensive sulfa drugs prevent infection but do not kill bacteria.

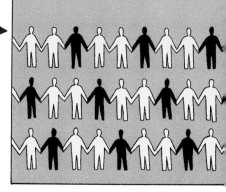

SUBSTANDARD LIVING CONDITIONS—overcrowded housing, poverty, and malnutrition—are breeding grounds for rheumatic fever. In a recent New York City study, two-thirds of the cases were found among poor people. Similar evidence was reported in Colorado.

A doctor should check every severe sore throat, especially in young children, by growing a culture from a throat swab. A Chicago study showed that 80 percent of the children treated for rheumatic fever for the first time could have avoided hospitalization through early diagnosis and prompt treatment.

Signs of rheumatic fever include pain or inflammation of the joints, poor appetite, fatigue, and fever. Signs of possible heart strain in adults who have had rheumatic fever are shortness of breath, excessive fatigue, or swollen ankles.

Many rheumatic-fever patients recover completely or are left with so little damage that they can be normally active, though they are always more susceptible to further attacks. As protection, high doses of penicillin must be given to adults as well as to children before an operation or a dental extraction.

VIRUSES may also damage the heart valves. In experiments, a virus called Coxsackie B has produced valve damage in mice. It has also been reported that some patients who have defective aortic and mitral valves do not have a history of rheumatic fever or bacterial endocarditis. Virus infections can cause inflammation of the myocardium as well as the lining tissue in newborn infants, apparently invading the fetal heart through the mother during pregnancy. Coxsackie B and other viruses are suspected causes of congenital heart defects.

CONGENITAL HEART DEFECTS are abnormalities existing in the fetal heart or in a major blood vessel near the heart at birth. Such defects, which occur both singly and in combination, may be a hole in the atrial or ventricular wall, an open connection between the the aorta and the pulmonary artery (patent ductus arteriosus, p. 107), narrowing of the heart valve (stenosis), or narrowing along the course of the aorta (coarctation, p. 108). These openings and/or obstructions may impair the infant's circulation, interfere with growth, reduce energy, and even endanger life. They generally increase the work of the heart. Some such defects cause an ever-increasing load, leading to cardiac enlargement, heart failure, and even death—mostly during infancy.

An estimated 30,000 to 40,000 babies are born annually in the U.S. with one or more such defects, sometimes traceable to German measles or other virus diseases but in most cases with unknown cause.

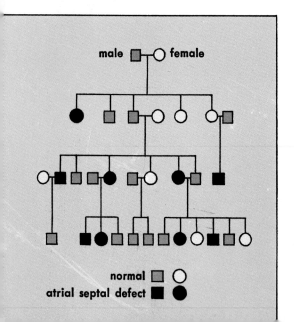

male ☐─○ female

normal ☐ ○
atrial septal defect ■ ●

HEREDITY is not generally considered a factor in congenital heart defects. Atrial septal defects occur in both sexes in consecutive generations, however, as shown in the three-generation diagram at the left. Also, patent ductus arteriosus has occurred along with gross abnormalities of the upper limbs in infants whose cells have an extra chromosome, the basic unit of heredity.

CLUES aid in detecting congenital heart defects in nearly all cases. If arterial blood mixes at any point with venous blood, it is relatively low in oxygen when it is delivered to the tissues. This is revealed by various signs and impaired functions: cyanosis (blueness of the mucous membranes); "blue baby" is the name generally given to the defect (technically, tetralogy of Fallot), but blueness may occur also in other heart defects.
- pallor of the skin
- undue fatigue
- inability to run or to play actively
- difficulty in breathing
- delayed growth
- failure to gain weight
- enlargement of the heart
- abnormal heart rate
- heart murmurs
- recurrent respiratory infections

Some of these signs may occur in other conditions, such as anemia, and diagnosis must be made by an exhaustive examination and special tests by a heart specialist. These include X-rays, fluoroscopy, blood tests, ECG, catheterization, and injection of radio-opaque fluid.

Structural defects of some congenital abnormalities (the trouble spots circled) are shown below and on pp. 109, 110.

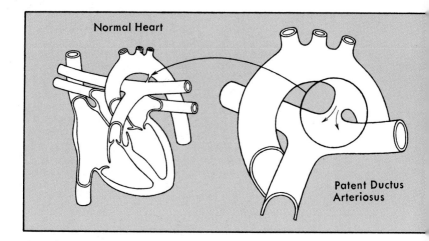

Normal Heart

Patent Ductus Arteriosus

PATENT DUCTUS ARTERIOSUS occurs when the fetal connection between the aorta and pulmonary artery fails to close shortly after birth. Some of the blood is shunted by the higher pressure in the aorta into the pulmonary artery. Instead of all the oxygenated blood going to nourish the body, some is wastefully recirculated through the lungs, putting a greater burden on the heart. The defect is corrected surgically by tying the open duct in two places and cutting between them.

COARCTATION OF THE AORTA is a narrowing or constriction of the vessel at some point after it issues from the heart. The flow of blood is obstructed, causing higher blood pressure in the head and arms and an increased workload on the left side of the heart. The narrowed section may be removed surgically, and the two ends sewn together. If the constricted area is large, a graft may be used to bridge the gap.

TETRALOGY OF FALLOT is a combination of four defects: (1) ventricular septal defect; (2) overriding aorta—that is, the aorta, instead of rising slowly from the left ventricle, straddles both ventricles just over the septal defect, thus receiving both oxygenated and unoxygenated blood; (3) pulmonary stenosis, obstructing the flow to the lungs; (4) enlarged right ventricle, due to overwork. The net result of the combined defects is that the tissues get insufficient oxygen.

Several operations are used to correct these malformations, though some only relieve their effects. In one, the pulmonary artery is joined with the right subclavian artery (under the collarbone), thus increasing the blood supply to the lungs. Complete correction of many of these malformations is now possible by open heart surgery.

SEPTAL DEFECTS may occur, in either the atria or the ventricles, with an opening in the septum between the right and left sides of the heart. If the hole is large, oxygenated blood from the left side is forced into the right side and then back to the lungs, as in patent ductus (p. 107). This causes the blood to recirculate wastefully and adds to the heart's work.

A septal defect in a ventricle means that the blood is forced through the hole in the septum into the right side of the heart, then back to the lungs under higher than normal pressure. The oxygenated blood that goes through the aorta is insufficient to nourish the body's cells. The heart overworks constantly to make up for this deficiency, and the extra load on the heart muscle may cause it to enlarge over a period of time.

An increase of pressure in the pulmonary artery may cause the blood to be shunted back to the left ventricle, which then pumps "mixed" or not fully oxygenated blood. Cyanosis—oxygen unsaturation—then occurs and can be detected in a bluish color change in the skin, in beds of the toenails and fingernails, and in the mucous membranes. Surgical closure restores the circulation to its normal course.

SURGICAL CORRECTION of an atrial septal defect may not be necessary if the hole is small and high up in the septum where it does not affect the circulation. A large hole allows the blood in the atria to mix, and the effect may be the same as that of a defective ventricular septum.

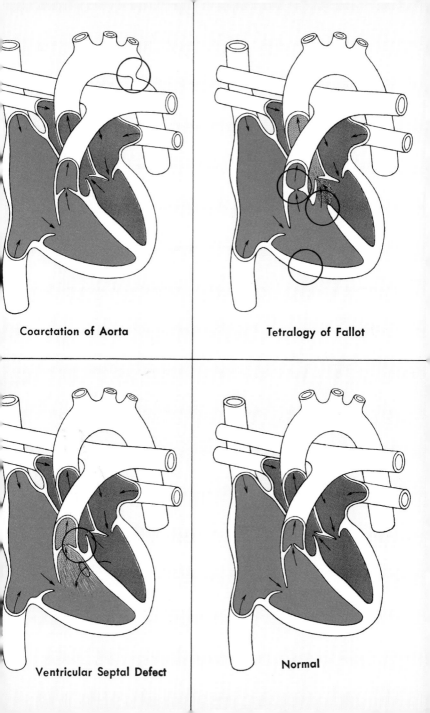

Coarctation of Aorta

Tetralogy of Fallot

Ventricular Septal Defect

Normal

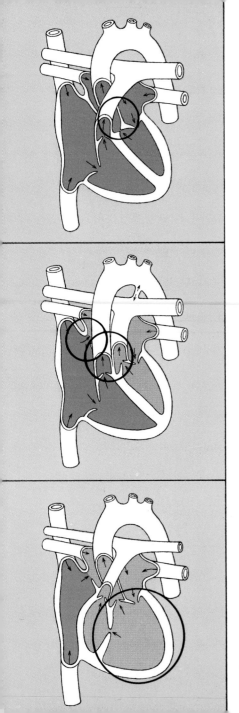

VALVULAR STENOSIS may involve either the aorta or pulmonary opening. The thickening of the valve or narrowing of the opening obstructs the flow of blood. The strain of pumping blood through the narrow valve may cause enlargement of both the atria and ventricles. In some cases, these defects can now be corrected by open-heart surgery.

TRANSPOSITION OF GREAT VESSELS is a defect in which the position of the two major arteries is reversed: the aorta issues from the right; the pulmonary artery from the left ventricle. Unless there is also an atrial septal defect or a patent ductus, allowing for some oxygenation, life would be impossible, as the two circuits are entirely separate. In some patients, two-stage surgery relieves the effects, or it may bring a complete cure.

A COMMON (OR SINGLE) VENTRICLE with pulmonary stenosis is a defect in which the heart is three-chambered, like the normal heart in reptiles and amphibians. The diagram of the defective heart shows a common ventricle—no opening from the right atrium and no tricuspid valve. Since the left ventricle pumps blood into both the aorta and the pulmonary artery, via a small opening (stenosed pulmonary artery), the ventricle is enlarged. Either the tricuspid or bicuspid valve may be closed, and the effect is inadequate oxygenation.

CONGENITAL MALFORMATIONS generally increase the heart's work. Surgical correction of such malformations has been performed successfully even in the first weeks of life, though the death rate is lower when surgery can be delayed until a later age. An operation can be avoided if the defect is mild and responds to control by drugs and constant medical care. The vulnerability of children to bacterial endocarditis infection (p. 104) is a special hazard. About 80 per cent of children with congenital heart defects can be either cured or helped to lead normal lives.

The decision to operate, and when to do it, depends upon a complete evaluation of each case, its peculiar risks, and on whether a complete or partial correction can be expected. Surgery may be postponed if there is a possibility that it may eventually prove unnecessary. In ventricular septal defects, the hole may close spontaneously or shrink sufficiently to allow efficient functioning with sustained medical care.

OPTIMUM AGES FOR SURGICAL CORRECTION OF CONGENITAL DEFECTS*

DEFECT	AGE IN YEARS
Coarctation of the aorta	6 to 12
Pulmonic stenosis with intact ventricular septal defect (dependent on right ventricular pressure)	3 or over
Aortic rings	Immediately
Patent ductus arteriosus (uncomplicated)	2 or over
Interventricular septal defects with large shunt	3 or over
Interatrial septal defects with large shunt	5 or over
Atrioventricular canals	2 or over
Total anomalous pulmonary venous return	Immediately
Tetralogy of Fallot—direct approach	5 or over
Transposition of great vessels	Immediately
Aortic stenosis (severe)	3 to 14

*Modified from McCue, C.M., *Pediatric Digest*, 6:35, 1964

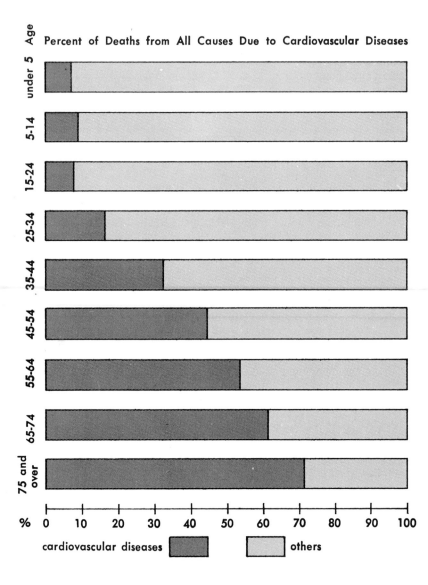

Age

Percent of Deaths from All Causes Due to Cardiovascular Diseases

cardiovascular diseases ▮ ▯ others

Death rates for cardiovascular diseases are shown in the above chart. All causes are as they were reported to the World Health Organization. The Chart compares cardiovascular diseases with other causes of death in different age groups. Proportion increases progressively with age.

112

CARDIOVASCULAR DISEASES (CV) account for 54.5 per cent of all deaths in the United States, claiming nearly a million lives annually. In 1900, these diseases were responsible for 20 per cent of all deaths in this country. Today, the United States has the highest death rate due to cardiovascular diseases of any country in the world.

DATA from the National Office of Vital Statistics show CV disease as the leading killer in the U.S. and also that diseases of the heart and blood vessels are the leading cause of death under age 65. Coronary disease alone accounts for about 30 per cent of deaths of men ages 45 to 54.

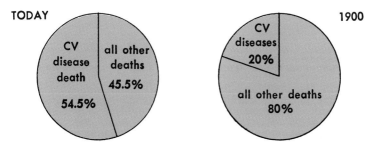

TODAY

CV disease death 54.5%

all other deaths 45.5%

1900

CV diseases 20%

all other deaths 80%

LEADING CAUSES OF DEATH AT ALL AGES

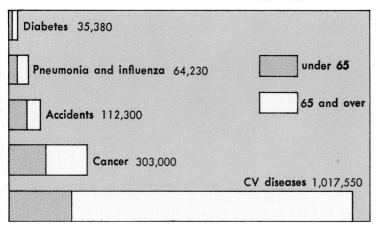

Diabetes 35,380

Pneumonia and influenza 64,230

Accidents 112,300

Cancer 303,000

CV diseases 1,017,550

under 65

65 and over

Estimated number of deaths in U.S. (1966) 1,869,000

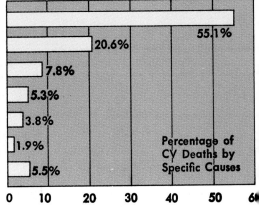

coronary heart disease	55.1%
stroke	20.6%
hypertension and hypertensive heart disease	7.8%
myocardial degeneration	5.3%
general arteriosclerosis	3.8%
rheumatic fever and rheumatic heart disease	1.9%
all other CV diseases	5.5%

Percentage of CV Deaths by Specific Causes

0 10 20 30 40 50 60

CORONARY HEART DISEASE (heart attack), as shown in the chart above, is by far the leading cause of death among cardiovascular diseases. It accounted for more than 669,829 deaths in 1969. Ranking second is stroke, the cause of 207,179 deaths. Together, as seen in the chart, heart attack and stroke are responsible for three-fourths of all deaths from CV disease. Congenital heart disease accounts for 8,000 deaths annually in children under five.

The chart below gives a breakdown of deaths due to cardiovascular disease by age. Note that about 25 percent of the deaths are in age groups under 65.

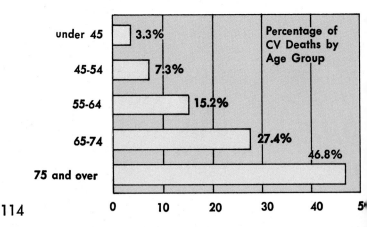

under 45	3.3%
45-54	7.3%
55-64	15.2%
65-74	27.4%
75 and over	46.8%

Percentage of CV Deaths by Age Group

0 10 20 30 40 50

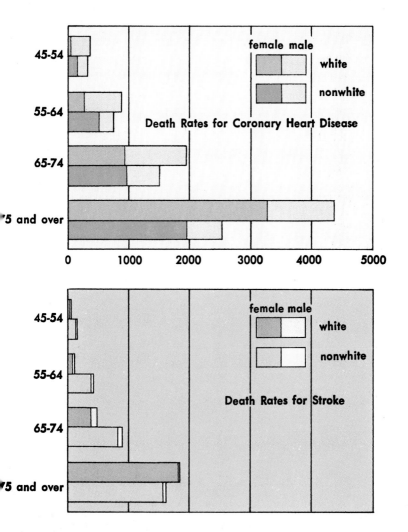

DEATH RATES BY SEX AND COLOR show that coronary disease death rates are higher among men than women, greater among whites than nonwhites. For white males, consistently higher; for white females, lower than for nonwhite, except in oldest age group. Death rates for stroke are higher in both sexes among nonwhites, except those over 75.

AT AGE 50, approximately one in every 100 men develops heart disease. If he shows two or three of the recognized high-risk factors (p. 90), his chances of having a heart attack before age 65 rise to 1 in 2, or 50 percent. Four decades ago, heart disease struck men mainly in their 60's; the present generation of males is struck mostly between 40 and 50.

When the deaths caused by accidents and suicides and those related to childbirth are eliminated (18 percent of the total), the death rate due to heart disease is roughly 70 percent, or 7 out of 10. People in the United States are living longer today than in 1900, however, so while the number of people dying is larger, the rate of death, or the number per 100,000 of the population succumbing to CV, is actually going down. People who would have died from tuberculosis, pneumonia, and typhoid years ago now live to the age when heart disease takes its greatest toll. A person who before the discovery of insulin in 1922 would have died from diabetes may now reach the age when most cardiac deaths occur. Also, 50 years ago a heart attack might have gone unrecognized and been recorded as acute indigestion, gall-bladder attack, or other disease. Thus, the trend that began in the 1950's is actually a small decline in the overall death rate for cardiovascular diseases at all ages. For men aged 45 to 64, the rate dropped by 6 percent. Steepest declines were from hypertension and hypertensive disease and from stroke. Only the coronary disease rate rose (4.3 percent).

Scientists and public health authorities believe the downward trend in the death rate from CV may be expected to continue. They point to developments that explain the first inroads into the major cause of death:

(1) advances in diagnosis and treatment of heart disease; (2) more vigorous efforts to rehabilitate the heart attack and stroke patient; (3) development of modern drugs to control hypertension, which has added productive years to many and reduced the risk of stroke—largely a complication of hypertension; (4) education of the public so that people seek medical advice earlier.

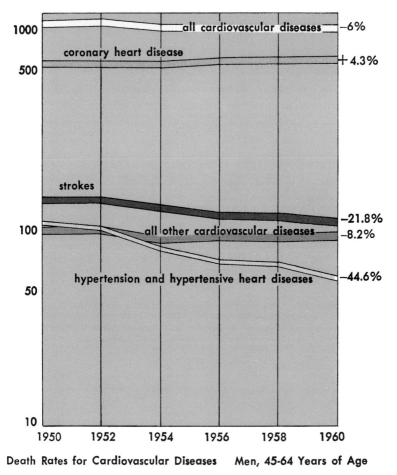

Death Rates for Cardiovascular Diseases   Men, 45-64 Years of Age

DETECTION

Some forms of heart disease can be prevented (pp. 124-147), a few cured, and almost all heart conditions fare better the earlier they are discovered and treated. A medical checkup once a year is minimum insurance against heart trouble. Sometimes a person is made aware of a heart condition for the first time when applying for an insurance policy or during an examination for military service or a new job, but rarely does heart disease come like "a bolt from the blue." The early signs of impending danger are often ignored. Through fear or the hope that they "will go away," they are attributed, through self-diagnosis, to another cause. Such clues call for an immediate visit to the doctor. If heart disease is ruled out, eliminating the fear is helpful.

WARNING SIGNALS include: (1) Shortness of breath on climbing stairs, running for a bus, or on awakening in the morning. (2) Pressing pains in the chest, especially on exertion or after meals. (3) Swelling of the legs and ankles and increased weight not due to habitual overeating. (4) Unusual fatigue with efforts that were previously undertaken with ease.

(5) Faintness and dizziness. (6) *Frequent* pounding headaches. (7) Ringing in the ears, palpitations, blurred vision, or nosebleeds. (8) Unaccustomed irritability, crossness, or impatience.

Some of these signs may *not* mean trouble, but only a doctor, not relatives or friends, can assess their significance in your particular case.

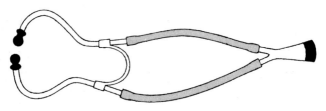

YOUR HEART CHECKUP is based on signs and symptoms that suggest possible trouble, as well as on medical tests. The doctor's examination often begins with a sizing-up of the patient; how he walks into the office, sits down, and relates his complaints, if any. He looks for signs of worry, uneasiness, or restlessness. An accurate patient's history is very important. The doctor's questions are designed to discover heart trouble or to rule it out as a cause of the complaints.

A PATIENT'S LIFE HISTORY helps in diagnosing his illness. His symptoms may be "warning signals" (p. 118) but do not necessarily indicate heart trouble. Fatigue, difficulty in breathing, and dizzy spells might be due to anemia, for example.

The doctor will ask the patient about previous illnesses—childhood infections as scarlet fever, rheumatic fever, and frequent sore throats; about his present state of health: does he spit up blood or have nosebleeds; is there hoarseness, pallor, or dryness of the skin; are there difficulties with swallowing, or pain in the abdomen or legs, especially after exercise; and has he gained or lost weight? The patient's habits of eating, drinking, sleeping, smoking, and exercise are important, as are his job and his attitude toward it, family or social stresses, and any drugs that he may have been taking. If his parents are dead, their ages and causes of death are relevant information.

Some of the answers (as well as the questions) may seem to have no bearing on cardiovascular disease. Others help in identifying a specific kind of CV trouble. Together, they give a picture of the patient's condition and future outlook.

In checking the pulse, listening to the heart and lungs, and taking the blood pressure the doctor takes the first steps toward a diagnosis. If the patient is frank when his history is taken and during the preliminary examination, the doctor may be able to give reassurance that the trouble has no serious cause. A patient's discomfort may be from nervous tension, indigestion, spasm of the esophagus, arthritis, or an infection, with no reason to suspect that the heart is not functioning properly.

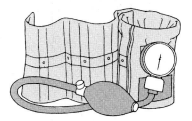

IF CARDIOVASCULAR DISEASE IS SUSPECTED, the doctor pursues his detective work, testing the work of every organ where things could go wrong (pp. 78-117). He also looks for the high-risk factors for heart disease (p. 90). The evidence he collects should enable him to rule out the suspicion of heart disease, or to confirm it.

EVIDENCE OF ABNORMALITY in the blood vessels may be revealed in the blood pressure. The doctor takes several readings and studies systolic pressure in reclining and standing positions and in the legs as well as in both arms to discover how the blood vessels and heart are responding to changes in posture. The readings also indicate where there may be constrictions obstructing the blood flow. A higher-than-average blood pressure, however, does not necessarily imply an abnormality if the blood supply seems adequate to the needs of the body without taxing the heart.

The doctor uses an ophthalmoscope to illuminate the interior of the eye and look at the network of the retinal blood vessels. In hypertension, the number of small arteries is reduced and they show constrictions and meanderings. In severe cases, there may be retinal hemorrhages and edema. Examination of other parts of the body may reveal a variety of information; discoloration of the skin, respiratory congestion, and swelling around the ankles are all clues to abnormalities.

KIDNEY FUNCTION is checked by routine urinalysis. This will show whether the kidneys are "leaking" albumin—an effect of high blood pressure. A dye —phenolsulfonphthalein (PSP)— is injected and its appearance in the urine timed to test the kidneys' efficiency in ridding the body of wastes. Normal kidneys excrete 25 to 50 percent of the dye in 15 minutes. Delayed excretion means abnormal function.

ECG's (p. 34) provide evidence of abnormalities not always revealed by physical examinations. If the ECG is normal, it can be used as a standard with which to compare any later changes. The tracing may show an S-T wave abnormality indicating "early" coronary disease, an enlarged left ventricle, or left-heart strain. The T-wave reflects the electrical change during the "recharging" or metabolic (restorative) phase of the ventricles. If depressed, it indicates an anemia of the heart. An ECG can show an undetected or "silent" heart attack, and lesser disturbances which do not show up in a routine physical examination.

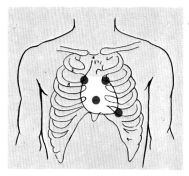

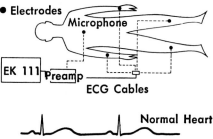

● Electrodes

Microphone

EK 111 Preamp

ECG Cables

Normal Heart

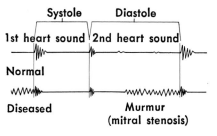

Systole   Diastole

1st heart sound   2nd heart sound

Normal

Diseased   Murmur
(mitral stenosis)

Red areas (above) show where heart murmurs are best heard. Diagram at top right shows points on body where electrodes of an electrocardiograph are attached, and a normal heart electrocardiogram. Diagram at bottom right shows phonocardiograms (sound recordings) of a normal heart and of a diseased heart with a murmur.

HEART SOUNDS ARE CLUES. If the first heart sound is very faint, myocardial weakness is suspected; a louder, second sound, depending on location, suggests increased pulmonary pressure. A split second sound indicates that the two semilunar valves are closing at different times.

Murmurs are noises of long duration superimposed on the normal heart sounds. They may be functional (p. 20) or due to a leaky, stenosed valve. When damaged A-V valves close incompletely, a systolic murmur is heard with the first sound. Damaged semilunar valves cause the second sound to become soft and hissing.

HEART SIZE AND POSITION are significant, too. The examination is done first by percussion, or finger-tapping. The doctor can distinguish between the hollow sound of the air-filled lungs and the dull and flat sound over the dense heart muscle. Thus, he gets a rough outline of the size of the heart. Fluoroscopic examination provides a more accurate idea of its size and position, as well as pumping and filling action. When recorded on film, it provides a permanent record, which may serve as a basis for future comparison. Such an examination generally includes four films taken at different degrees of rotation.

121

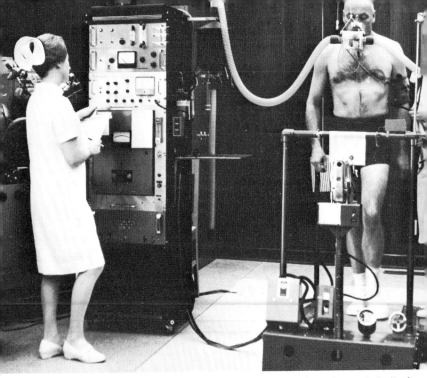

The treadmill technique of exercising as shown here is used similarly to the Master two-step test descibed below.

THE MASTER TWO-STEP TEST checks the heart function after exercise. A person with coronary artery disease may have a normal ECG when lying down if his heart is functioning adequately to supply his resting needs, but an abnormality may show up after exercise.

The test is made on a specially constructed, two-step platform, each step 9 inches high and 20 inches wide. The patient climbs onto the platform, walks down the other side, then turns around and crosses the platform again. The number of trips taken in the "single test"

(1½ minutes) or the "double test" (3 minutes) has been standardized according to age, sex, and height. The patient is told to stop at first sign of chest pain or discomfort.

An ECG is taken directly after the exercise is completed. The photograph shows a modified method in which the ECG is followed continuously during the exercise by means of electrodes attached to the patient. The main advantage of this method is its greater safety, as any changes can be detected before the patient reports pain.

LABORATORY TESTS are used for confirmation, to identify the type of heart disease, to determine the extent of damage, if any, and to follow the response of the disease to treatment. Some tests need to be repeated under different conditions: before breakfast, after a test meal, or on different days. (Certain symptoms involving the digestive system or metabolism may confuse diagnosis.) Each test adds to the accuracy of diagnosis in doubtful cases and helps to locate the trouble.

BLOOD TESTS are done to find signs of anemia and to determine sugar, cholesterol, and aldosterone content. A high blood sugar indicates diabetes; high cholesterol indicates an underactive thyroid gland. High sodium and low potassium probably mean an excess of aldosterone, which raises blood pressure and interferes with kidney function (p. 124). A specific antibody reaction helps in diagnosing rheumatic fever.

Other heart ailments may be identified by testing the sedimentation rate. A rise in transaminases (enzymes normally present in small quantities in blood serum) indicates that damage to heart muscle has occurred after infarction.

ANGIOCARDIOGRAPHY, one of the newest procedures for examining the heart and blood vessels, helps to locate trouble areas precisely. An opaque, sometimes colored, or radioactive substance is injected into a vein or introduced by a catheter (p. 41). The opaque material intensifies the X-ray or fluoroscopic image.

Cineoangiocardiography is a modification of this method, making use of motion-picture photography to study the heart's chambers and valves in action. The identifiable (colored or radioactive) substances permit the determination of cardiac output, stroke volume, arterial tone, the extent of valve leakage, and blood shunts.

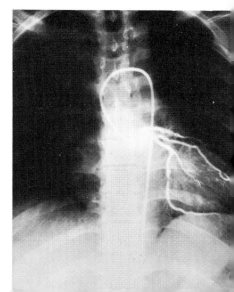

REMEDIAL ACTION

Some heart diseases can be cured by treatment, some can be relieved, and some prevented. Treatments include surgery, the use of various drugs, and modifications in the patient's living habits—in diet, physical activity, and the avoidance of stress.

DRUGS vary in kind and in the way they work, each acting specifically and at a particular trouble spot.

DIURETICS help rid the body of excess water and salts; they lower blood volume and, in turn, blood pressure. Excretion of salt reduces the need for salt restriction in the diet. Diuretics block the reabsorption by the kidney tubules of salt filtered out by kidney.

Thiazides (chlorothiazide, for example) are synthetic diuretics that were developed during the middle 1950's. They also reduce the quantities of other antihypertensive drugs needed.

Side effects from modern diuretics are few. Since potassium as well as sodium salts may be excreted in excess, causing muscle weakness, this effect is counteracted by prescribing potassium salts.

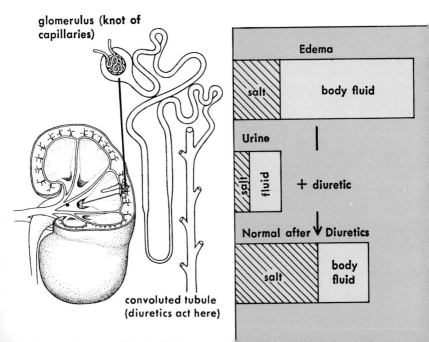

glomerulus (knot of capillaries)

convoluted tubule (diuretics act here)

Edema

salt | body fluid

Urine

salt | fluid | + diuretic

Normal after ↓ Diuretics

salt | body fluid

ANTIHYPERTENSIVE DRUGS lower blood pressure. Some act by reducing the activity of the sympathetic nervous system. This relaxes the blood vessels and increases the blood flow through the smaller vessels. Others, acting like chemical nerve cutters, prevent release, or interrupt the flow, of norepinephrine, or NE (p. 101), at nerve terminals in the arterial wall. Some deplete NE stored in the brain.

These drugs often have side effects such as heartburn, nausea, stuffy nose, dizziness, and drowsiness. Faintness and dizziness may result from an excessive lowering of the blood pressure. To avoid or minimize side effects, smaller amounts of two or more drugs may be prescribed in combination.

Antihypertensive drugs are not cures, but their power to lower blood pressure can check advance of atherosclerosis in damaging heart and blood vessels. Control of hypertension has been a major achievement in heart disease control.

VERATRUM ALKALOIDS are drugs that stimulate the afferent nerve endings in the right atrium (R.A.). Through reflex action, the vasoconstrictor center is inhibited and fewer impulses are discharged to the arteries, causing vasodilation.

ERGOT makes blood vessels less sensitive to the action of NE.

ENZYME INHIBITORS block NE production.

GUANETHIDINE is a synthetic drug that prevents NE release at the nerve endings in the arterial wall.

RESERPINE drains or depletes the storage sites of NE in the brain and the arterial wall.

GANGLION BLOCKERS are synthetic drugs that interrupt the transmission of neurohormones at sympathetic ganglia.

Main Sites of Drug Action

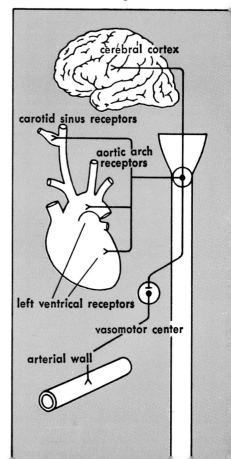

cerebral cortex

carotid sinus receptors

aortic arch receptors

left ventrical receptors

vasomotor center

arterial wall

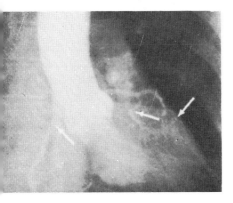

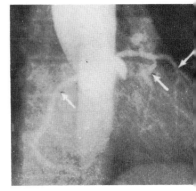

| Before | After |

CORONARY VASODILATORS include nitroglycerine (p. 88), which rapidly relieves anginal pain, and many other nitrates that act more slowly to widen the coronary vessels and increase the flow of blood to the heart muscle. They lessen the work of the heart by reducing the myocardium's oxygen requirement and relieving the local anemia.

The coronary arteriogram (X-ray picture) shows the coronary arteries before and after use of a vasodilator, indicating a widening of the coronary channels. An ECG would show at what point a coronary vasodilator becomes effective.

Foxglove

DIGITALIS, a drug obtained from the foxglove plant, has been in use for over 150 years. It strengthens and lengthens the heart's systole and favors excretion of excess body water. Digitalis is used in congestive heart failure along with diuretics and other drugs. In excess, however, digitalis may itself be toxic to the heart, producing irregular rhythms (see ECG chart).

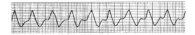

Ventricular tachycardia due to digitalis excess.

ANTICOAGULANTS prolong the time the blood takes to clot. In healthy blood vessels, blood remains fluid (unclotted), but hypertension and atherosclerosis damage the arteries and may set off the clotting process. Anticoagulants lessen the danger of a thrombus or embolus (p. 86) blocking the blood flow. They may be given to patients after a coronary occlusion or a myocardial infarction. The risk of a hemorrhage from slow clotting is weighed against the advantage of prolonging clotting time. Persons taking anticoagulants must have periodic laboratory tests to check on clotting time and on amount of prothrombin (a clotting substance) in their blood.

Heparin- and coumarin-type compounds are two kinds of anticoagulant drugs. Heparin is formed naturally in the liver; coumarins are produced in the laboratory. Heparin is injected into the blood and acts promptly. It is used only in emergencies because its action is short-lived. Coumarins, given orally, are used in long-term preventive treatments. The physician decides which drug is best, depending on patient's history, condition, and ability to cooperate, and on facilities.

The patient is instructed also about the hazards of taking aspirin, vitamin "tonics," antibiotics, or other drugs at the same time as these drugs. He must, of course, tell his dentist he is taking anticoagulants before he undergoes dental surgery. With the proper precautions, periodic testing, and alertness to signs of bleeding, complications are rare.

QUINIDINE is a myocardial depressant. It is used in auricular fibrillation to restore normal rhythm. Since a fibrillating heart is alrady depressed and its circulation compromised, digitalis is usually given first to slow down the rate to "condition" the myocardium.

TRANQUILIZING DRUGS are given to reduce tension and anxiety in cardiac patients. Anger, worry, and distress increase the heart rate and blood pressure, and, in general, disrupt heart function. Thus, they may precipitate an anginal attack. Calming patient reduces risk.

prothrombin
+
calcium
↓
thrombin

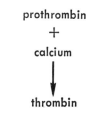

thrombin + calcium + fibrinogen → fibrin = clot

127

SURGERY on the heart has been the most dramatic life-saving advance in the treatment of cardiovascular disease. Today, surgery is done on veins (varicose), on the great arteries issuing from the heart, the coronary vessels, vessels supplying the brain and kidneys, and also on the heart and its valves. The techniques are numerous and varied. Some operations on the heart require opening the chest only; others involve opening the heart.

ARTERIAL REPAIR may be necessary if blood flow in key arteries is blocked by a thrombus (atherosclerotic narrowing of the channel) or by a congenital constriction of the arterial wall (coarctation of the aorta, p. 108). An obstructing clot may be removed by one of two ways: (A) the aorta may be cut open, and a spoon-shaped instrument inserted into the coronary artery past the clot, which is then scraped out; or (B) the coronary artery may be cut open directly between two sutures or ties and the clot removed. The artery is widened by a patch graft stitched over the opening. The hazard of interrupting the blood flow to the heart is overcome by placing the patch on the blood vessel before opening it (C). The patch and the arterial wall are then slit (D), and the slit edges of the patch are clamped. Blood flow is thus restored quickly. The incision in the artery remains open (E) even after repair is completed.

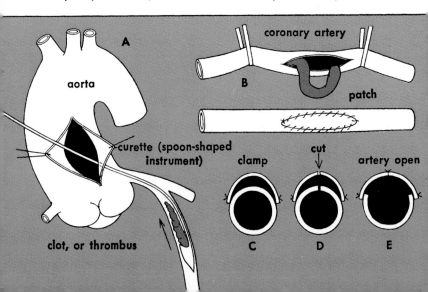

A

coronary artery

aorta

B

patch

curette (spoon-shaped instrument)

cut

clamp

artery open

clot, or thrombus

C   D   E

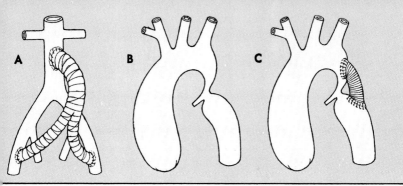

BYPASS GRAFT is used in an artery with an atherosclerotic plaque, which has been located by X-ray arteriography. The obstructed section, left in place, is bypassed with a synthetic graft. The section of the abdominal aorta shown above (A) is narrowed by atherosclerosis where it branches to form the iliac and has been bypassed by the graft. A similar correction for aortic coarctation is shown in illustrations B and C.

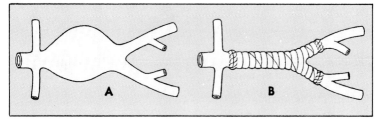

REPLACEMENT GRAFTS are used in treating aneurysms. The weakened arterial wall, ballooning out to the point of rupture, is removed and replaced with a patch graft, shown here before correction (A) and with a replacement graft (B).

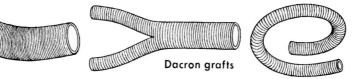

Dacron grafts

BLOOD-VESSEL GRAFTS were once made with pieces removed from cadavers. Such transplants served as a framework until the patient's own new tissue grew to replace it. Today, the best material for synthetic replacement has proved to be knitted Dacron. Sections of flexible tube of various diameters (1/4" to 1") and shapes are cut, and can be fitted without fraying. They are strong, durable, **and do not interreact with body.**

129

**MAINTAINING CIRCULATION DURING CARDIOVAS-
CULAR SURGERY** is important, as only a few minutes
without blood can be permanently damaging to some
tissues. Some blood-vessel grafts (an artery in an arm
or a leg, for example) can be done without cutting off
the blood supply to vital organs. Correction of a patent
ductus arteriosus (p. 107) can be done also without
clamping off a major artery. The surgeon uses the so-
called "blind" or "closed" method, locating the pul-
sating vessel with his finger. He then lifts it up, places
two sutures under it, and ties them.

In operations on the aorta, on an artery to the
brain, or on a kidney, blood vessels can be clamped
for only a short time. If only one of the four arteries
to the brain is to be repaired, the remaining vessels
furnish the brain with blood. In other areas, a temporary shunt around the operative site prevents interrupting the circulation.

In operations on the thoracic aorta and on the
heart itself, shunts are not feasible. Open-heart surgery to correct defects in the heart's chambers was
made possible by invention of heart-lung machine, in
1953, with which the surgeon can undertake complicated surgical procedures lasting several hours. He can
open the heart, empty it of blood so that his vision is
unimpeded, and operate unhurriedly.

THE HEART-LUNG MACHINE
enables the cardiac surgeon to
operate on a "bloodless" heart,
for the machine takes over the
heart's pumping action and the
lungs' oxygenating function. The
bloodstream temporarily bypasses both vital organs.

Two sterilized plastic tubes
(catheters) are inserted into the
venae cavae to divert blood
from the heart into the artificial
pump. The blood flows down to
the bottom of the oxygenator
tube, placed 18 to 24 inches below level of patient's heart,
picking up a supply of oxygen
as it flows through the mixing
chamber that also admits large
bubbles of oxygen from a tank.

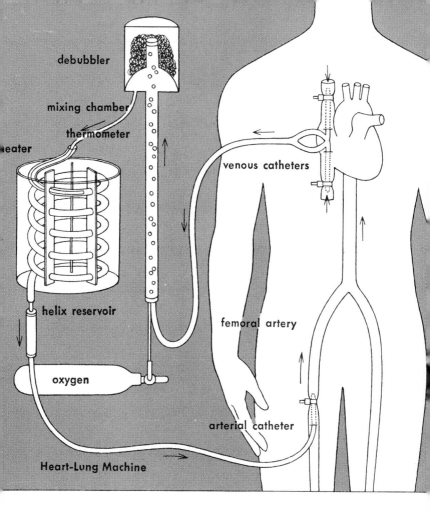

Heart-Lung Machine

The bubbles lift the blood through the mixing chamber to the debubbler, where excess bubbles, which could cause embolism, are removed. Sponges in the debubbler chamber filter out any clots.

Gravity pulls the blood down to the helix reservoir, a coil of plastic tubing holding a one-minute supply of oxygenated blood maintained at body temperature by a thermostatically controlled water bath. A pump returns the blood through the patient's femoral artery (in the thigh). When blood reaches the venae cavae, it is intercepted by plastic catheters, and circuit is repeated.

OPEN-HEART SURGERY saves an increasing number of children from premature death and is lengthening the useful lives of many adults. Cardiac surgeons can now correct formerly inoperable congenital heart defects, repair valves damaged by diseases such as rheumatic fever, and even restore the circulation of the heart itself when it has been impaired by coronary artery disease. The operations are done on a "bloodless" heart, with the mechanical pump and oxygenator taking over for the bypassed heart and lungs, extending the operating time and increasing accuracy.

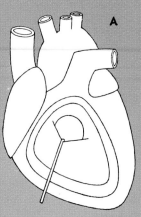

REPAIR OF SEPTAL DEFECTS involves closing a hole between the atria or ventricles which is present at birth (p. 106). The diagrams here show the three stages in the repair of a ventricular septal defect. The heart is open and a plastic patch cut to size is in place (A). Sutures are then placed around the margin of the hole and are run through the edge of the patch (B). The patch is secured in place by the sutures (C).

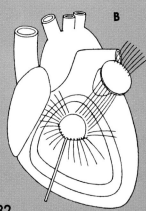

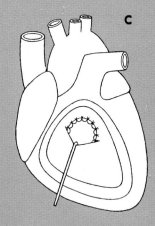

REPAIR OF LEAKY HEART VALVES that permit backflow of blood is done by stitching a three-leafed valve into a two-leafed one, or sewing a piece of plastic material along the edge of the defective leaflet to extend it. The valves most often damaged are the aortic and mitral valves (left ventricle).

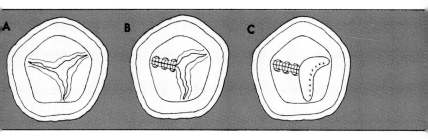

A leaky aortic valve (A) does not close completely. The two leaflets are sewn together (B) and the remaining gap is eliminated by attaching a plastic patch (C).

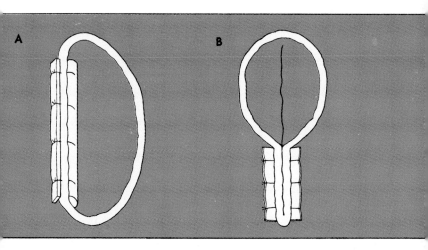

A MITRAL VALVE is repaired by inserting a plastic cushion where the leaflet tissue is lost (A), shortening the circumference of the opening. One end of the stretched ring is stitched to make the opening smaller (as shown at B). Constriction of the valve, is sometimes corrected without opening the heart. A finger thrust firmly downwards through the opening slits the leaflets apart, enlarging the opening. More complex mitral operations are done with the heart open.

133

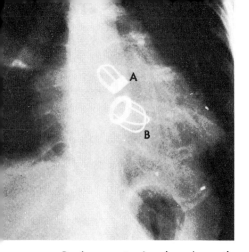

ARTIFICIAL HEART VALVES pose many problems in design, construction and insertion. The first such mechanism, the Starr-Edwards "ball-in-a-cage", consists of a silicone rubber ball inside a metal cage. The ball is free to bounce back and forth as the pressure of the blood changes. Early successes with aortic valve replacements were not immediately followed by similar successes in replacing diseased mitral valves, primarily because of increased risk of blood clot formation. Improved valve design and materials have helped to reduce this problem. Floating disc valves appear to have performance and safety advantages over ball valves, especially as replacements for the mitral and tricuspid valves. As a result, their clinical use is increasing rapidly.

Replacement of valves by artificial ones (prostheses) is sometimes necessary. Two complete one-way valves of the ball type are shown after replacing an aortic valve (A) and a mitral valve (B), as seen by x-ray or fluoroscope.

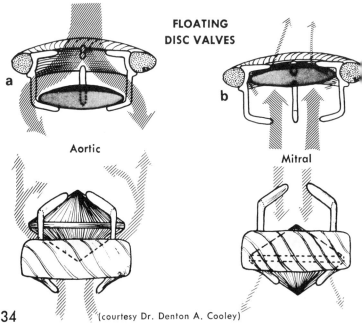

FLOATING DISC VALVES

a

Aortic

b

Mitral

134   (courtesy Dr. Denton A. Cooley)

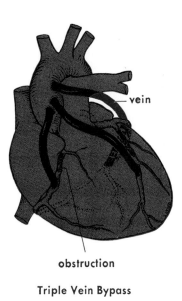

vein

obstruction

Triple Vein Bypass

Most patients require multiple vein grafts. The left anterior descending coronary artery usually is the most important site of bypass; the dominant right coronary artery the most common site of bypass.

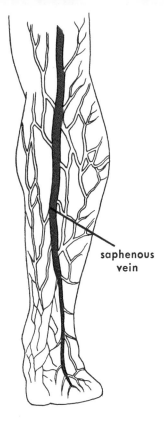

saphenous vein

REVASCULARIZATION, when the heart is impaired by atherosclerotic coronary disease, (p. 84), is a recent innovation in the treatment of occlusive disease. There are two operative approaches. One is a direct approach to remove a segmental stenosis in a major coronary artery thereby restoring normal circulation to the distal arterial bed. The second method is an indirect approach based upon the implantation of a systemic vessel into the myocardium for the treatment of heart disease.

Almost all revascularization today is done by direct surgery upon the coronary arteries using the bypass principle. Thus, surgeons are using veins, usually the saphenous vein from the leg as a bypass graft or swinging down the internal mammary artery for direct anastomoses to the coronary vessels distal to the point of arteriosclerotic narrowing. This surgery is possible only because of the recent demonstration of arteriography, a special technique of visualizing coronary arteries.

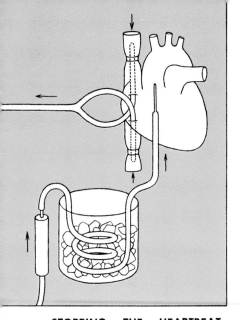

rently, the heart is stopped by clamping the aorta past the aortic valve and coronary arteries' openings. Deprived of blood the heart stops, a state of cardiac arrest reverses when the clamp is released. The bloodless heart is protected by having been cooled.

HYPOTHERMIA (lowered body temperature) occurs when the heart is cooled to 65° F. This not only stops its beat but also lowers the oxygen consumption, thus preventing damage to cells due to insufficient oxygen. If the heart's temperature and oxygen supply become too low, the conducting system fails, and rhythm becomes disordered.

STOPPING THE HEARTBEAT, or elective cardiac arrest, is a technique sometimes used to make more accurate repairs possible. Depressant drugs, such as potassium salts or acetylcholine will stop the heart beating, but chilling the heart is a preferable procedure. This is done by hooking a plastic cooling coil (see diagram), immersed in a tub of crushed ice, into the heart-lung machine circuit. Cur-

After the surgical work is completed and the ties have been removed from the vessels, the blood is permitted to flow through the heart again. The heart resumes its beat with the flow of warm blood. But sometimes it fails to take up its normal rhythm and shows signs of fibrillation as the heart muscles contract independently, each at its own rate. A fibrillating heart cannot expel blood effectively, and the condition is rapidly fatal if not corrected.

An electric defibrillator (see left, wires in position) must be used immediately. This instrument delivers a single, large impulse of electric current, depolarizing the electric current in all the fibers of the myocardium at the same time. If a heart block occurs, an external pacemaker can be used to restore normal rhythm (p. 138).

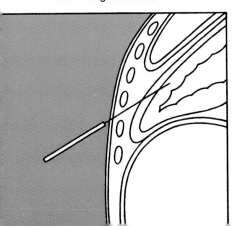

AUXILIARY PUMP is a means of maintaining an adequate blood supply to patients who require surgery but who are poor surgical risks. Their hearts, weakened by previous coronary occlusions, fail to pump strongly enough to keep up a normal blood pressure. They cannot withstand the rigors of an opened chest nor the bypass procedure in using the heart-lung machine. To aid the heart, an auxiliary pump is used as an artificial pulse. It automatically withdraws and delivers a precise volume of the patient's blood during each cardiac cycle. The pump's rhythmical action is electronically controlled. Installation requires only the exposure of the femoral arteries.

TWO TUBES, one inserted in each femoral artery, are attached to the pump. At the beginning of each systole, the pump withdraws a measured quantity of blood. At the beginning of diastole, it returns the same amount of blood into the circulation. The effect is to reduce the work of the heart in opening the aortic valve in systole, to sustain an adequate arterial pressure, and to provide a steady blood flow to the vessels during diastole. By lowering the aortic pressure just prior to systole, the pump avoids the load that the heart normally has in overcoming the resistance in the arterial tree.

The pump is triggered into motion by the heart's electrical activity at the onset of the *R* wave in the ECG (early systole). As a result, the pump actually operates in counter rhythm to the heart cycle.

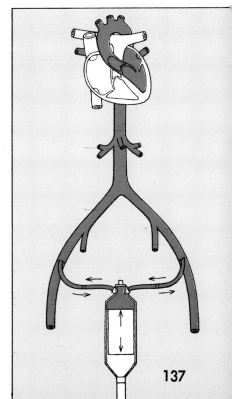

137

ARTIFICIAL PACEMAKERS are used chiefly for patients with chronic heart block who live with the constant threat of a sudden failure of the ventricles to put out blood. This may be due to a recurrent cessation of systole or to a disordered flutter or fibrillating beat. A cessation of circulation for a minute, or even less, causes dizziness, distress, and unconciousness. Unless the heart beat is restored, death occurs.

An artificial pacemaker delivers repeated, evenly spaced, electrical impulses to the heart. If the electrodes of the pacemaker are applied to the skin of the chest, a current of high voltage is necessary. This powerful stimulus is painful and cannot be continued for long. Because an external pacemaker of this sort can be put into operation quickly, it is used in emergency resuscitation of cardiac patients. Internal permanent pacemakers are installed surgically in persons with chronic heart block. More than 60,000 Americans now "wear" pacemakers. Experimentation to solve the problem of renewing batteries, has resulted in the successful implantation of nuclear-powered pacemakers, with an expected lifetime of at least 10 years.

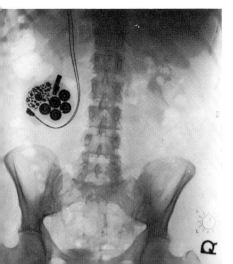

ELECTRODES of permanent pacemakers are implanted in the myocardium or on the pericardium; or, contained in a catheter, they are inserted into the ventricle. Wires run through the chest from the electrodes to a battery-powered source that delivers tiny pulses of electricity to the heart muscle. Pacemakers differ in operation and in the position of their power source. In some, the power source is carried in a sling worn around the neck.

THE R-F PACEMAKER works by a remote-control, radio-frequency device. Only the receiver is implanted. A transistorized transmitter which fits into a jacket pocket is connected by a thin cable to a circular broadcasting antenna held to skin with an adhesive. Signals are broadcast to receiver.

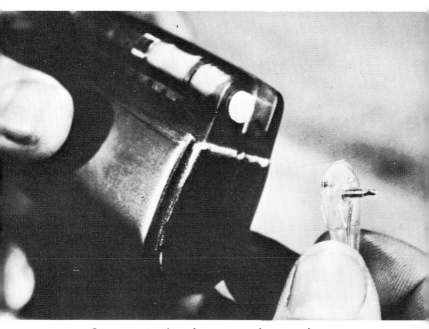

Components of nuclear-powered pacemaker

TOTALLY IMPLANTED PACE-MAKERS are most widely used. The power source is inserted under the skin, usually of the abdomen. Wires run from the electrodes through a tunnel under the skin to the electronic power package. The device (p. 138), contained in a hermetically sealed silicone rubber case, weighs 4 ounces and is small (1½″ x 2½″ x ½″).

The unit contains tiny mercury cell batteries and transistors. Designed for small size, high reliability, and low power drain, it has an expected life of 3 to 5 years. When the batteries wear out, they can be replaced by opening the abdominal skin under a local anesthetic. The pacemaker operates at rate of 60 to 70 beats a minute.

Devices now in use discharge impulses in step with those emitted by the natural pacesetter. During exercise, excitement, or after meals, the rate is automatically stepped up, but this takes more power.

ARTIFICIAL HEARTS, completely mechanical, have kept dogs and calves alive for short periods of time, and a partially artificial heart has been successfully used in a human being. Several models of artificial hearts have been designed in laboratories in the United States, Argentina, and Japan. The ultimate goal is a totally implantable (inside the chest) device, including a power supply, that will approximate the workings of the natural heart and replace a dying patient's failing heart. Research emphasis today, however, is on booster pumps and living transplants.

THE SAC-TYPE HEART is made of an inner flexible sac (ventricle) inside a rigid housing, powered by compressed air from an outside pump. In the diagrams below, the sac (A) is in diastole, filled with blood. In systole (B), air has been introduced between the two walls, causing the inner wall to collapse, expelling the blood. This pumping action is achieved by the alternate compression and expansion of the blood in the sac, which in turn is due to the pulsing entry and exit of pressured air. One-directional blood flow is achieved by a built-in leaflet or ball-type valve in the silicone rubber sac.

An operation for installing an artificial heart is feasible. During the replacement procedure, the circulation can be maintained by the heart-lung machine, or the patient can be cooled (by hypothermia) while replacement is made.

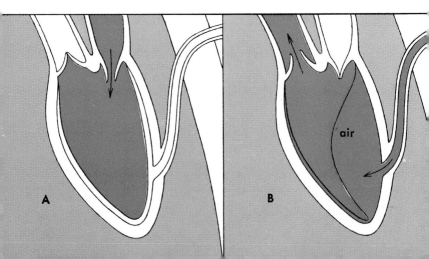

THE IMPLANTABLE BYPASS is a "half-heart" replacement. The artificial inflow tube is stitched into the left atrium and the outflow tube into the thoracic aorta (A). The blood bypasses the faulty left ventricle, flowing from the atrium directly into the aorta. The flexible bypass, contained inside a rigid container, is sutured to the body wall. Compressed air is pulsed into the space between the inner and outer walls of the bypass, which is illustrated in the section diagram to the right during diastole and systole (B). Good results have followed the use of this device in a few cases.

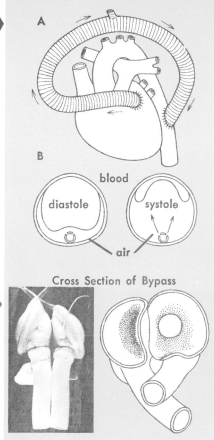

A

B

blood

diastole

systole

air

Cross Section of Bypass

BOTH VENTRICLES are replaced in the artificial heart illustrated here. A silicone rubber (Silastic) sac fitted with a ball valve is inserted into each ventricle. The air tubes to the pump emerge through the atria. The blood-vessel connections are similar to the kinds that are used in the implantable bypass.

UNSOLVED PROBLEMS, common to all these experimental models are: (1) construction materials, (2) driving mechanism for permanent implantation, (3) source of energy, and (4) regulating devices.

The material for the sac must be elastic, strong, and long-lived, and able to withstand the chemical action of the body fluids without injuring the patient's tissues, neither causing blood clots nor destroying red blood cells. The driving mechanism must be small enough to fit inside the chest and generate sufficient power to drive the blood. Among the energy sources studied are: electrical; electromagnetic; and a combination of electrical and skeletal muscle power, utilizing a shoulder muscle harness to drive air bellows (beneath skin of chest) and stimulated through its nerve by a device similar to an implantable pacemaker.

141

REHABILITATING THE CORONARY PATIENT begins as soon as the critical period after an "attack" has passed. Today, 5 out of 7 recover, including those who have subsequent attacks. Many people lead normal lives, and most return to their jobs. Some don't even require adjustments in their work and way of life.

THE FIRST HOURS AND DAYS after a coronary are critical, 85 per cent of deaths from coronaries occurring within the first week. Emergency medications are used directly after the attack, but there are no "wonder" drugs for this period and the patient is kept under intensive care in a special coronary unit, which greatly improves his chances of survival.

Electronic equipment continuously monitors temperature, pulse rate, respiration, blood pressure, and ECG, and records them on an oscilloscope. Electric impulses are flashed on a screen and signal an alarm if anything goes wrong. The oscilloscope may be connected with an external pacemaker and a defibrillator for immediate heart resuscitation. An oxygen mask and equipment for intravenous use of drugs are at hand.

Damaged parts of the heart are never restored but are replaced by scar tissue. The heart begins its repair work immediately: the obstructed artery is bypassed, new channels open up, and old ones become enlarged. During this period, treatment consists mainly of prolonged rest and watchfulness for complications such as pulmonary edema, shock, fever, and the life-threatening erratic rhythms and ventricular standstill.

Electronic equipment monitors patient's condition.

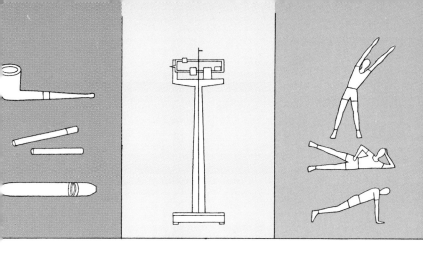

THE REHABILITATION PRO-GRAM begins as soon as the critical days are over. **To** strengthen the heart, the patient needs supervised exercise—not **inactivity.** As soon as he is able, he sits in an armchair for eating, reading, and simple, prescribed exercises. Closely supervised, early movement of all the joints prevents complications and favors physical and emotional recovery. The patient is taught to increase his capacity for self-help gradually. The exercises progress to walking measured distances on the level, later on stairs.

The goal is to restore the patient to productive work which in some cases may mean new employment. Some cities have established Cardiac Work Evaluation Clinics that contribute greatly to satisfactory vocational rehabilitation. For the patient able to resume his former work a balance between work, recreation, and rest is prescribed. He is advised to stop smoking, keep his weight down, to eat four small meals daily, to get plenty of rest and to take moderate exercise, avoiding overexertion.

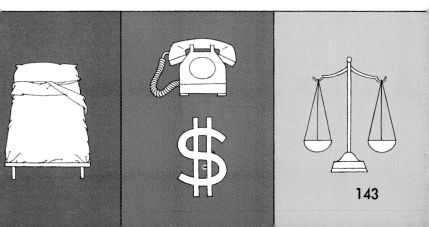

REHABILITATING THE STROKE PATIENT depends partly on the efforts put forth by the stroke victim himself, partly on professional care and guidance, and partly on the cooperation he receives from his family. Most persons who have had a stroke survive, some living for many years. A great many, however, are disabled by paralysis, wasting of muscles, and sometimes loss of speech. Beginning while the patient is in the hospital and later at home, much can be done to prevent or to keep at a minimum the permanent crippling that follows damage to parts of the brain. The key to the stroke patient's recovery is planned use of the affected limbs as soon as possible after the stroke. The aim is to help him regain much of his lost independence.

CRIPPLING occurs because, after a stroke, the muscles that straighten the fingers, hands, legs, and other parts of the body are weakened. The flexing muscles pull these parts into a bent position, where they remain. If nothing is done to prevent it, these muscles continue to tighten, and the joints become stiff. Meanwhile, the straightening muscles grow still weaker and waste away.

The doctor plans exercise treatment, and the physical therapist or nurse helps the patient to carry them out. The family is also instructed on how to care for the patient when he returns home. The damage can be increased if the wrong exercises are used or by delay in starting therapy. The patient should not be pushed beyond his capacity at any stage.

Specific instructions to guide the family step-by-step through progressive exercises are available through government and private agencies (p. 152). These include recommended height and width of single-sized bed for easy access in moving the patient, type of mattress, etc.

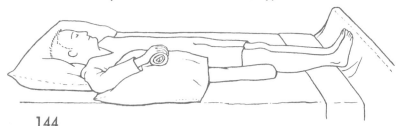

EXERCISES are begun as soon as the patient is ready. Both arms and legs are exercised the same number of times to prevent the muscles on the normal side from becoming weak through disuse. Hand exercise steps are shown above.

When the patient is able to stand and take first steps, he may need supports for safety and security. At first, he will hold onto chairs or sofas and later use a cane for walking. Handrails, or grab bars, can be installed in corridors.

A variety of devices are used to encourage the patient to help himself in eating, bathing, dressing, and grooming. Reading, writing, telephoning, and preparing food unaided are similarly made possible by specially designed devices.

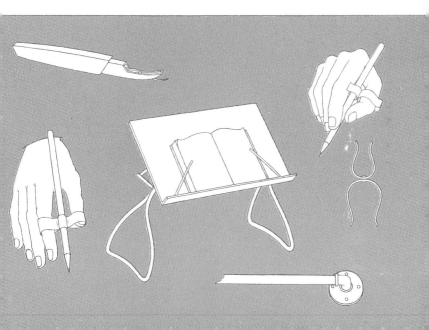

RESEARCH ACHIEVEMENTS

The last two decades have produced a 7 percent drop in the cardiovascular death rate among middle-aged men. Investigations have been carried on in medical research centers and hospitals, in pharmaceutical laboratories, and in universities by scientists, physicians, electronic engineers, and laboratory technicians. Independent researchers, teams working together on special projects, and collaborating laboratories have contributed their resources and energies to the prevention and treatment of heart disease.

Fundamental questions, such as inheritance patterns which might lead to birth defects, have been examined by chemists working on embryos in chicken eggs. And practical solutions are also a part of current cardiovascular research: A gelatin seal to make a synthetic artery wall leakproof during healing; revolutionary ideas in electronics as an implantable nuclear-powered engine to drive an artificial heart; a pacemaker powered by the body's own energy.

Research achievements also include an improved method of diagnosing septal defects. A catheter is inserted through a vein into the right ventricle, and the patient then takes a single breath of freon, a colorless refrigerant gas. If a hole exists in the septum, a detecting device connected to the catheter will register the appearance of the freon in the ventricle.

Examination of medical records of 50,000 male students revealed that among the stroke victims all showed high blood pressure, cigarette smoking, short stature, early parental death, heart "awareness," and non-participation in varsity sports. Continuing research is essential.

THE ATTACK ON HEART DISEASE is many-sided. Cardiovascular disease was designated an epidemic in the United States by the American Heart Association and research took on new dimensions.

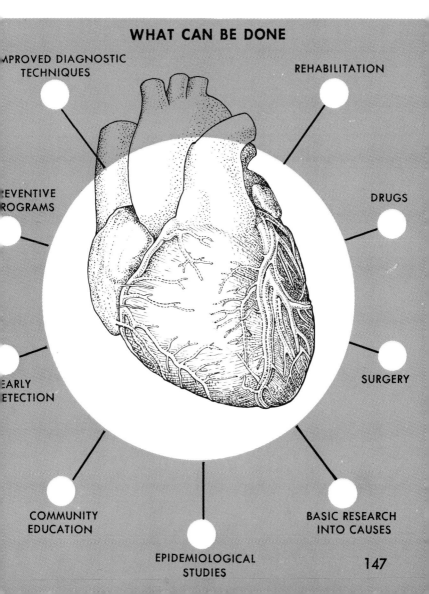

WHAT CAN BE DONE

IMPROVED DIAGNOSTIC TECHNIQUES

REHABILITATION

PREVENTIVE PROGRAMS

DRUGS

EARLY DETECTION

SURGERY

COMMUNITY EDUCATION

EPIDEMIOLOGICAL STUDIES

BASIC RESEARCH INTO CAUSES

147

HEART TRANSPLANTS constitute a new frontier in the struggle to overcome heart disease, yet research is continuously demanded. After years of animal tests by researchers, Dr. Christiaan N. Barnard, a South African surgeon, performed the first such transplant in 1967 on a 55-year-old man; the patient died 18 days later. Since then, there have been numerous transplants, and several patients have lived for more than four years after the operation. A heart-lung machine

SURGICAL TECHNIQUE

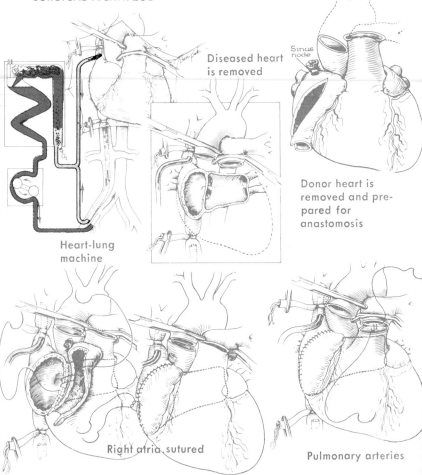

Diseased heart is removed

Sinus node

Donor heart is removed and prepared for anastomosis

Heart-lung machine

Right atria sutured

Pulmonary arteries

takes over the functions of pumping and oxygenating the blood normally done by the heart and lungs, while surgeons remove the diseased heart. Then the donated heart is sutured to the blood vessels. In selecting a donor, red and white blood cells of donor and recipient must be as compatible as possible. In addition to obtaining consent of the donor's family, physicians must rule the donor dead (i.e., the brain must be considered dead) before removal of the heart.

(courtesy Dr. Denton A. Cooley)

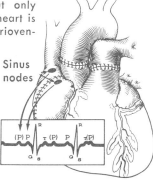

Left atria joined

Both sinoauricular nodes remain intact, but only impulse in donor heart is transmitted to atrioventricular node.

Sinus nodes

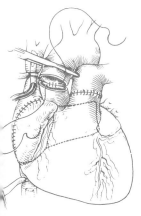

nd aortae joined

149

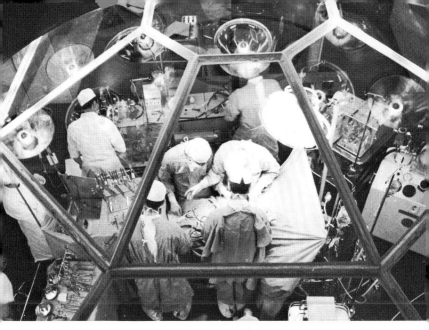

Modern operating room

THE MYSTERY OF REJECTION is another area of research being explored because the immunological system of the body is the chief problem, causing the deaths among the majority of the recipients of heart transplants. Contained within the transplanted heart are protein substances called antigens. These—as would invading bacteria or viruses—provoke a defensive response by the recipient's body; other protein molecules called antibodies, plus white blood cells, rush to attack the transplant. To overcome this rejection mechanism, surgeons use various drugs, among them a drug called azathioprine. The suppression, in turn, makes the recipient susceptible to infections. Thus, the patient with the transplanted heart confronts rejection or infection. Other problems include the high cost of the operation (the average cost is estimated at about $18,700) and postoperative care.

150

NEW DRUGS are being studied by researchers in the United States and Europe. Among them are urokinase and streptokinase. Urokinase, which is derived from human urine, is hard to produce and is very expensive. Streptokinase, derived from streptococcal bacteria, was used before urokinase, and has been criticized as difficult to handle. Urokinase, by activating a blood substance called plasminogen, launches a sequence of events leading to the dissolution of recently formed clots. A drug called clofibrate has been used to treat angina patients. There have been tests in England and Scotland involving 1,214 patients over a five-year period. Physicians report that clofibrate may prevent heart attacks in patients but that the drug does not seem to be effective in patients who have already had one attack.

OTHER THERAPEUTIC TECHNIQUES being studied and used include a coronary bypass surgical procedure, and special drugs, one type for dissolving blood clots, and another for treating angina pectoris by lowering high levels of cholesterol and other fatty substances. A total of 35,000 of these bypass operations have been performed since 1967, reaching a peak of 20,000 in 1972.

The patient with a clogged artery must first undergo coronary arteriography and catheterization. These involve infusing an opaque dye into the vessels and penetration of the vessels by the catheter in order to locate the exact site of the obstruction. The heart-lung machine is used to carry out the pumping and oxygenation of the blood. Surgeons remove a leg vein, suture it to the aorta, and connect the vein to the coronary vessel, bypassing the obstruction.

EDUCATION

About the year 1900, public information media began to focus attention on the grim fact that heart disease was the No. 1 killer in the U.S. They pointed out also that with each advance in diagnostic techniques, in emergency care, and medical and surgical treatment, lives were being saved and cardiac patients rehabilitated. Then a more hopeful note was sounded: Most people with heart disease can live happy and productive lives. Research into basic causes coupled with the concrete fact of a drop (if small) in the death rate among men made it possible to spread an even more cheerful message: It is possible now to reduce the risk of heart attack.

STATISTICS are still alarming. In 1969 for example, 54 percent of deaths in the U.S. were from cardiovascular disease, 21,-790,000 adults suffered from high blood pressure, and 27,-130,000 were estimated to have cardiovascular disease.

Control of cardiovascular disease now seems to be in sight, but success depends partly on education. People must be made aware through all available media that the individual risk of heart attack and stroke can be reduced. Examples of this kind of campaign can be seen in the American Heart Association's series of sketches that pinpoint risk factors.

SAFEGUARDS TO

Keep Weight Down   Decrease Saturated Fats   Stop Smoking

COMMUNITY PROGRAMS are being developed in a concerted effort to reduce the death toll from cardio-vascular disease. Many national organizations, some with widely different interests, are cooperating. Newspapers, magazines, radio and television networks, as well as schools and industry are all aiding in campaigns to reduce risk and advise against smoking. Some examples are given below.

SYSTEMATIC SCREENING of school children may detect strep infections and aid in preventing rheumatic heart disease. Children are also screened for suspicious heart murmurs and are referred to their doctors.

VOCATIONAL REHABILITATION AGENCIES assist the stroke patient, giving physical and occupational therapy, and providing devices and appliances. The work capacity of heart patients is estimated by Cardiac Work Evaluation Units to help them in returning to self-supporting jobs. Counseling, which helps him to find a suitable occupation, is also provided.

DISTRIBUTION OF EDUCATIONAL MATERIALS prepared by the American Heart Association (pp. 154-155) is a valuable service. Information on surgical techniques, new drugs, diet control, and physical activity is translated into everyday language to increase public understanding of the heart problem and to help change attitudes toward heart disease. These materials clear up misconceptions and give hope to heart patients.

CAMPAIGNS in schools and among parent and community groups are designed to discourage cigarette smoking in young people.

REDUCE RISKS

Control High
Blood Pressure   Regular Exercise   Avoid Tensions

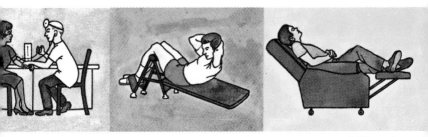

THE AMERICAN HEART ASSOCIATION, organized in 1942 with headquarters in New York City, operates through 55 affiliates, one in each state, plus Puerto Rico, Chicago, Washington, and St. Louis. The AHA is financed by public contributions to the Heart Fund. About $10,000,000 annually (over one-third of the fund) is allocated to research, distributed chiefly as grants-in-aid to qualified scientists. This is the largest single nongovernmental support for this type of research. The rest, excluding administrative expenses, goes for public health education, professional education and training, community services, and field studies.

PUBLIC EDUCATION by the AHA includes preparation and distribution of booklets that give authoritative information on every aspect of the heart problem—congenital heart disease, hypertension, angina, rheumatic fever, stroke, and others. The titles of some of these helpful booklets are *Facts About the Heart and Blood Vessel Diseases, Planning Fat-Controlled Meals, After a Coronary, Anti-Coagulants, Your Physician and You,* **and *Diet and Heart Disease.***

Every Heart Association maintains a Heart Information Service to answer questions on heart-related subjects—where and how to seek help for a child requiring surgery, or obtain material needed for a school science project.

The AHA also spearheads campaigns against smoking, preventive programs in industry, programs on nutrition, on stroke rehabilitation, on prevention of rheumatic heart disease, and dozens of others.

MEDICAL EDUCATION by the AHA includes the publication of four professional periodicals, the conducting of annual scientific meetings and exhibits, courses, films, and self-testing exhibits. All make new knowledge on cardiovascular disease accessible to the nation's physicians. More than 80,000 physicians, dentists, and nurses were trained in the life-saving technique of external heart massage to revive a stopped heart. A survey five years later revealed that one-fourth of the persons on whom it was used were saved, and so the AHA announced that in cooperation with three other organizations, the training could be extended to policemen, firemen, lifeguards, and ski and highway patrol personnel.

GOVERNMENT AND VOLUNTARY AGENCIES are in the forefront of the mounting attack on heart disease. These are principally the National Heart Institute, a Division of the National Institutes of Health, the U.S. Public Health Service, both under the U.S. Department of Health, Education, and Welfare; and the American Heart Association, a voluntary professional organization, and its affiliates. To a degree, their activities overlap. Both, for example, sponsor research, conduct community programs and services, and engage in public educational campaigns. The AHA, however, carries by far the greater burden of each.

THE NATIONAL HEART INSTITUTE places special emphasis on basic research. Studies are done both by NHI scientists and by those working under government grants in research centers, universities, and hospitals. A sampling of subjects under investigation includes the body's synthesis of cholesterol; the value of low-fat diets; effects of drugs that may lower blood cholesterol; the effect of hormones on the release of tissue fat into the blood; how drugs act to lower blood pressure; how enzymes inactivate norepinephrine and other blood pressure-raising hormones; cardiac catheterization studies to detect heart shunts; drugs to dissolve blood clots; designing instruments to locate accurately the heart's conduction system.

Results of these studies have an important bearing on causes, diagnosis, and treatment of atherosclerotic heart disease, hypertension, and stroke.

THE PUBLIC HEALTH SERVICE is continuing the Framingham study (p. 90) which pinpointed the factors in the development and progression of coronary heart disease. Its National Diet-Heart Feasibility Study placed 1,500 men on an experimental diet of modified foods designed to lower blood cholesterol. The study may be extended to include 100,000 persons.

THE HEART DISEASE CONTROL PROGRAM provides professional, technical and financial assistance to state and local health departments for applying available knowledge in the control and prevention of heart diseases. It introduced a new method (fluorescent antibody) for quick identification of the strep organism that causes rheumatic fever. To make it widely available, the Public Health Service provided courses to train technicians in its use and alerted physicians to its availability.

MORE INFORMATION

American Heart Association, THE AMERICAN HEART ASSOCIATION COOKBOOK, David McKay Co., Inc., N.Y., 1973.

Amosoff, Nikolai M., M.D., THE OPEN HEART, Simon & Schuster, Inc., N.Y., 1967.

Barnard, Christiaan N., M.D., HEART ATTACK: YOU DON'T HAVE TO DIE, Delacorte Press, Dell Publishing Co., Inc., N.Y., 1972.

Bennett, Iva, and Martha Simon, THE PRUDENT DIET, David White, Inc., N.Y., 1973.

Blakeslee, Alton L., and Jeremiah Stamler, M.D., YOUR HEART HAS NINE LIVES: NINE STEPS TO HEART HEALTH, Prentice-Hall, Inc., Englewood Cliffs, N.J., 1964.

Blumenfeld, Arthur, HEART ATTACK: ARE YOU A CANDIDATE, Paul S. Eriksson, Inc., N.Y. 1964.

Boylan, Brian Richard, THE NEW HEART, Chilton Book Co., Philadelphia, Pa., 1969.

Brams, William A., M.D., YOUR BLOOD PRESSURE AND HOW TO LIVE WITH IT, J. B. Lippincott Co., Philadelphia, 1956.

Harrison, Charles Y., THANK GOD FOR MY HEART ATTACK, Holt, Rinehart & Winston (College Dept.), N.Y., 1949.

Maule, Tex, RUNNING SCARRED: THE ODYSSEY OF A HEART ATTACK VICTIM'S JOGGING BACK TO HEALTH, Saturday Review Press, N.Y., 1972.

Miller, Robert A., M.D., HOW TO LIVE WITH A HEART ATTACK.

Poole, Lynn and Gray, I AM A CHRONIC CARDIAC, Dodd, Mead & Co., N.Y., 1964.

Riedman, Sarah R., YOUR BLOOD AND YOU. THE STORY OF CIRCULATION, Abelard-Schuman Ltd., N.Y., 1963.

Seltzer, Arthur, THE HEART, ITS FUNCTION IN HEALTH AND DISEASE, University of California Press, Calif., 1966.

Williams, Harley, M.D., LIVING WITH YOUR HEART, Henry Regnery Co., Chicago, Ill. 1971.

INDEX

Accelerator nerves, 44, 46, 47, 68
Acetylcholine, 67, 68, 138
Adenosine triphosphate, 39
Adrenal gland, 80, 81, 83
Adrenalin, 49, 67, 68, 81, 92, 97
Adventitia, 62
Age, as risk factor in heart disease, 96
Air sacs in lungs, 52, 53, 97
Albany, 93
Aldosterone, 82, 83, 123
"All or none" principle, 29
Alveoli, 52
American Heart Association, 99, 146, 152, 153, 154, 155
Amphibians, 10
Anatomy of heart, 6
chambers of, 8, 13, 15
endocardium, 7
muscle, 26
myocardium, 7, 126
pericardium, 7
septum, 8
valves of, 16
Anemia, 88, 123
Aneurysm, 86, 98, 99, 129
Angina pectoris, 68, 87, 88, 126, 151
in legs, 100
Angiotensin, 82
Anticoagulants, 100, 127
Anticoronary Club, 95
Antihypertensive drugs, 125
Aorta, 16, 19, 22, 48, 59, 66, 70, 74, 83, 86, 106, 107, 108, 110, 130
Aortic coarctation, 83
Argentina, 140

Arteriogram, coronary, 126, 151
Arterioles, 52, 60, 70, 71
narrowing, 81
thickening of walls, 97
Artery, 60, 62, 63, 71, 80
repair, 128
Asthma, 78
Astronauts, 77
Atherosclerosis, 83, 84, 85, 86, 87, 92, 93, 94, 95, 96, 97, 98, 99, 100, 125, 127, 128, 129, 135
ATP, 39
Atria, 8, 9, 15, 17, 18, 19, 29, 30, 31, 33, 45, 54, 59, 110
Atrioventricular (A-V) valves, 16, 17, 19
Auricles, 8, 9, 15, 30, 31
Auriculo-ventricular (A-V) node, 30, 31
Auscultation, 21
Autonomic nervous system, 44
A-V bundle, 30
node, 30, 31
Auxiliary pump, 137

Bacterial endocarditis, 104, 111
Barnard, Dr. Christiaan N., 148
Bicuspid valve, 16, 110
Birds, 10
Blood, flow, 64, 70
output by heart, 40
quantity per minute, 4
sound of, 20
volume of, 12, 73
Blood vessels, 60, 61, 62 63
control of diameter, 65
grafts, 129

regulation of size, 64
structural alterations in, 83
Blood pressure, 74, 75, 77, 92
"Blue baby," 107
Brain, 44
Bright's disease, 82
Bronchi, 52, 97
Bronchiole, 52

Cancer, 93
Capillaries, 13, 52, 53, 57, 58, 60, 61, 67, 70, 97
rate of flow in, 71
Carbon dioxide, 49, 58
Cardiac output, 40
changes in, 42
measurement of, 40
reserve, 42
Cardiovascular disease (CV) and death rate, 113, 114, 115, 116, 128
Cardiovascular-renal disease, 78
Cardiovascular surgery, 130
maintaining circulation, 130
Carotid sinus, 48, 66
Catheter, 39, 41, 107, 123, 130, 151
Chambers of heart, 8, 9
thickness of walls, 15
Chicago, 93, 105
Chlorothiazide, 124
Cholesterol, 84, 85, 86, 90, 91, 92, 93, 94, 95, 96, 97, 123
Chordae tendineae, 16
Cineoangiocardio-graphy, 123
Circulation time, 72
Circulatory system, 50
coronary, 54
fetal, 58
portal, 57
pulmonary, 52

Clofibrate, 151
Closed circulatory
    system, 10
Clot, 86, 87, 98, 127
Coarctation, 83, 106,
    108, 111
Cold-blooded animals,
    10
Collateral circulation, 97
Colorado, 105
Congenital heart
    defects, 106, 107
    "blue baby," 107
    coarctation of aorta,
      106, 108
    common ventricle, 110
    cyanosis, 107, 108
    disease, 114
    increase work on
      heart, 111
    patent ductus
      arteriosus, 106, 107
    septal defects, 108
    stenosis, 100
    surgical corrections,
      111
    tetralogy of Fallot,
      107, 108, 111
    transposition of great
      vessels, 110
    valvular stenosis, 110
Congestive heart
    failure, 89
Coronary arteries, 54,
    55, 68, 86, 87, 88,
    128, 136
    arteriogram, 126
    bypass, 151
    circulation, 39, 54, 68
    heart attack, 87, 90,
      114, 115, 116
    sinus, 9, 19, 54
    vasodilators, 126
Corticosteroids, 67
Coumarin, 127
Cournand, 41
Coxsackie B, 105
Crippling, 144
Cyanosis, 107, 108
Cycle of heart, 18, 19

Defibrillator, 136
Depressor nerves, 44,
    48, 66, 81

Detection of heart
    disease, 118, 119,
      120, 121
    angiocardiography,
      123
    blood tests, 123
    checkups, 119
    ECG, 121
    heart sounds, 121
    laboratory tests, 123
    life history of patient,
      119
    master two-step test,
      122
    warning signals, 119
Diabetes, 93, 96, 100
Diastole, 18, 19, 22, 36,
    68, 75, 77
Diastolic pressure, 80
Diet, 95
Digestive organs,
    circulation to, 57
Digitalis, 126
Diuretics, 89, 124
Ductus arteriosus, 58

ECG, 32, 34, 35, 36, 89,
    90, 107, 121, 122,
    126, 137
Education, 152
Einthoven, Willem, 32,
    34
EKG, 32, 34
Electricity generated in
    heart, 32, 33
Electrocardiogram, 32,
    34, 89
Electrocardiograph, 32,
    34, 35
Embolus, 127
    cerebral, 98
Emotional stress, 90, 92
Emphysema, 78
Endocardium, 7
Energy output of heart,
    38
    needs of heart, 39
Enzyme inhibitors, 125
Epinephrine, 68, 81, 83
Ergot, 125
Estrogen, 96
Exercise, 97

Fat, 85, 86, 92, 94, 95,

    96, 97
Femoral artery, 130, 137
Fetal circulation, 58, 59
Fetus, 58
Fibrillation, 28, 36, 127
Fibrin, 84
Fish, 10
Flowmeter, 69
Fluoroscope, 89, 107,
    121
Food, 39
Foramen ovale, 58
Forssmann, 41
Framingham, 90, 93

Gangrene, 84, 100
Ganglion blockers, 125
German measles, 106
Grafts, 129
Guanethidine, 125

Hales, Stephen, 76
Hardening of arteries,
    84
Heart, adaptability, 38
    anatomy of, 6
    artificial, 140
    beat, 4, 18
    capacity of, 15
    chambers of, 8, 9
    circulatory system, 12
    cycle, 18, 19
    damage, 78
    defects, 78
    disease, 78
    double pump, 13
    electricity generated
      in, 32, 33
    energy needs, 39
    energy output, 39
    enlarged, 78
    fibrillation, 28
    laws of, 29
    muscle, 26, 27, 28, 54
    nodes, 30
    output of blood, 40
    pacemaker, 31
    position, 6, 121
    pulse, 22, 23, 24, 25
    pumping power, 15
    quantity of blood
      pumped, 4
    rate of, 4, 22, 23, 24,
      25, 31

research, 147
rhythmicity, 28, 89
shape, 6
size, 4, 121
sounds, 20
surgery, 128, 130
thickness of walls, 15
transplants, 148
valves, 16
Heart attack, 87, 114, 115, 116
Heartbeat, 18, 37, 136
Heart block, partial, 89
Heat disease, 78, 95
    age as risk factor, 96
    congenital, 106, 107
    coronary, 114
    damage due to rheumatic fever, 105
    overweight, 96
    physical inactivity, 97
    sex as risk factor, 96
    smoking, 97
Heart-lung machine, 130, 136
Heparin, 127
Hepatic artery, 57
Heredity and heart defects, 106
High blood pressure, 80, 90, 92
Hypertension, 78, 80, 81, 82, 83, 92, 96, 98, 101, 120, 125, 127
    anti-drugs, 125
Hypertrophy, 78
Hypotension, 101
Hypothermia, 136, 140

Infections, 102
Inferior vena cava, 57, 59
Intermittent claudication, 100
Intima, 62

Japan, 91, 140

Kidney disease, 78, 80, 82
Korean War, 96
Kymograph, 27, 28

Lactic acid, 39, 67, 68
Laennec, René-Théophile, 21
Laws of heart, 29
Leaky heart valves, repair of, 133
Lipids, 94
Lipoproteins, 84, 94
Liver, 57
Los Angeles, 93
Low blood pressure, 101

Mammals, 10
Massachusetts, Framingham, 90, 93
Media, 62
Medulla, 44, 45, 47
Minnesota, University of, 91
Minute volume, 40
Mitral valves, 16
    repair, 133
"Murmurs," 103, 121
Muscle, heart, 26
    compared to skeletal, 26
    electricity generated by, 32, 33
    energy output, 38
    needs, 39
Myocardial infarction, 87, 127
Myocardium, 7, 126, 135

National Heart Institute, 155
National Institute of Health, 155
National Office of Vital Statistics, 113
Nephrosis, 93
Nerves, cardiac, 44
    remote controls, 49
    vasomotor, 65
New York City, 95, 105
New York, Westchester, 92
Nicotine, 97
Nitroglycerine, 88, 126
Nodes, 30
Norepinephrine, 81, 83, 101, 125

Obesity, 96
Open-heart surgery, 132
Overweight and heart disease, 90, 96
Oxygen, 39

Pacemakers, artificial, 138
Papillae, 16
Parasympathetic nervous system, 44
Patent ductus arteriosus, 106, 107, 111, 130
Penicillin, 104, 105
Pericardium, 7
Phenolsulfonphthalein (PSP), 120
Pheochromocytoma, 83
Phonocardiograph, 32
Phospholipids, 94
Physical inactivity, 97
Placenta, 58, 59
Plaques, 84, 95, 92, 129
Plasminogen, 151
Portal circulation, 57
    vein, 57
Position of heart, 6
Pressor nerves, 48
Prevention of heart disease, 118
Public Health Service, 90, 95, 99, 155
Pulmonary artery, 9, 16, 19, 52, 58, 106, 107, 108, 110
    circulation, 52
    veins, 9, 52
Pulse, 22
    pressure, 75
    rate, 23, 125
    taking your own, 23
    variation, 23, 24, 25

Quinidine, 127

Rate of heartbeat, 4, 22
Red blood cells, 61
Rehabilitation of coronary patient, 142
    of stroke patient, 99, 144
Rejection of transplant, 150

159

Remedial action, 124
Reptiles, 10
Research, 147
Reserpine, 125
Revascularization, 135
Rheumatic fever, 102,
    105, 123
  control of, 104
Rhythm of heart, 4, 28,
    136
Richards, 41

S-A node, 30, 31, 33, 45
Scarlet fever, 102
Semilunar valves, 16,
    17, 19
  leaky, 103
Septum, 8, 15, 30, 54,
    58, 59, 108, 111,
    132
Sex as risk factor in
    heart disease, 96
Shape of heart, 6
Sino-auricular (S-A)
    node, 30, 31
Size of heart, 4
Skeletal muscle, 26
Smoking, 90, 92, 97
Sounds of heart, 20
Sphygmomanometer, 76
Starling's Law, 29
Starr-Edwards ball, 134
Stenosis, 103, 106, 108,
    110, 111, 121
Stethoscope, 21
Streptococcal infections,
    102
  control of, 104
Streptokinase, 151

Stroke, 84, 98, 99, 144
Stroke volume, 40
Surgery, cardiovascular,
    128, 135
Sympathetic nervous
    system, 44, 68
Syphilis, 102
Systemic circulation, 53
Systole, 18, 19, 22, 32,
    68, 75, 77

Temporal artery, 23
Tetralogy of Fallot,
    107, 108, 111
Thiazides, 124
Thromboangiitis
    obliterans, 100
Thrombus, 86, 87, 98,
    127
Thyroid gland, 97, 127
Thyroxin, 49
Tibial artery, 23
Trachea, 52
Tranquilizing drugs, 127
Transaminases, 123
Tricuspid valve, 16, 110
Triglycerides, 94, 97
Tuberculosis, 93

Ulcers, 93
Umbilical arteries, 59
  veins, 59
U. S. Dept. of Health,
    Education, and
    Welfare, 155
Urokinase, 151

Vagus nerve, 44, 45, 46
    47, 68

Valves, 16, 20, 63
  damaged by disease,
    103
  leaky, 42, 43
  repair, 133
  replacement, 134
Valvular stenosis, 110
Varicose veins, 101, 128
Vasoconstrictor nerves,
    65, 68, 82, 125
Vasodilator nerves, 65,
    68, 126
Vasomotor nerves, 65,
    66, 67, 81
Veins, 60, 62, 63, 67,
    71, 101
Vena cava, 9, 19, 54,
    130
Ventricles, 8, 9, 14, 15,
    17, 19, 20, 29, 30,
    31, 108, 110, 141
  systole, 8, 19, 22, 36
Venules, 60
Veratrum alkaloids, 125
Vertebrates, 10
Viruses, 105
Volume of blood, 12

Warm-blooded animals,
    10
White, Dr. Paul Dudley,
    97
Windpipe, 52
World Health
    Organization, 112

X-rays, 107

Yugoslavia, 91